When Retirement Goes Bad
LIFE SUCKS

The Hidden Defect in Your Retirement Portfolio That Everyone Wants to Ignore

Kerry Morris, CFP®, CFEd®

HUGO HOUSE PUBLISHERS, LTD.

When Retirement Goes Bad–Life Sucks
The Hidden Defect Everyone Wants to Ignore

©2022. Kerry Morris. All rights reserved.
No part of this book may be reproduced or transmitted in any form or by any means, electronic or mechanical, including photocopying, recording, or by an information storage and retrieval system without written permission of the publisher.

Certified Financial Planner Board of Standards, Inc. (CFP Board) owns the certification marks CFP®, CERTIFIED FINANCIAL PLANNER™, and CFP® (with plaque design) in the United States, which it authorizes use of by individuals who successfully complete CFP Board's initial and ongoing certification requirements.

DISCLAIMER: The information provided in this book is for informational purposes only and is not intended to be a source of advice or tax analysis with respect to the material presented. The information and/or documents contained in this book do not constitute legal or financial advice and should never be used without first consulting with a financial professional to determine what may be best for your individual needs. Content contained or made available through this book is not intended to and does not constitute legal advice or investment advice.

The publisher and the author do not make any guarantee or other promise as to any results that may be obtained from using the contents of this book. You should never make any investment decision without first consulting with your own financial advisor and conducting your own research and due diligence.

To the maximum extent permitted by law, the publisher and the author disclaim any and all liability in the event any information, commentary, analysis, opinions, advice and/or recommendations contained in this book prove to be inaccurate, incomplete or unreliable, or result in any investment or other losses.

ISBN: 978-1-948261-68-5

Library of Congress Control Number: 2022907143

Cover Design & Interior Layout; Ronda Taylor, www.heartworkcreative.com

Hugo House Publishers, Ltd.
Austin, TX • Denver, CO
www.HugoHousePublishers.com

*To Mom and Dad
for your unstoppable belief in me,
constant encouragement, and persistent prayers.
Your faith in Jesus that you passed to me became my own.
He is the Rock of my life.*

Contents

Foreword vii

Introduction—Finding the Right Solution ix

   1 Think This Can't Happen to You? 1

   2 What Really Matters 11

   3 The Perfect Couple: Tom and Sarah 23

   4 The Danger Zone—The Four Lines that Define the High Cost of Aging 29

   5 The Widow Wiped Out Physically and Financially 39

   6 Be a Care Manager Not a Care Giver 45

   7 The High Rollers 51

   8 Patsy and Her Mom 63

9   The Defective Portfolio Syndrome 73

Acknowledgements 97

About the Author 99

Introduction—
Finding the Right Solution

THE PROBLEM WAS ALWAYS *RIGHT THERE*. THERE WAS never enough money. People who had elderly parents, wives who were taking care of their husbands (or vice versa), or good friends who were concerned about their friend or neighbor, or if they were the appointed caregiver, it didn't matter. They were all there because they heard that maybe—hopefully—I could help them.

This was in 2010, and I was deep in the trenches of elder-care planning. I felt for them. I had become an investment advisor and founded Assurance Financial Partners two years prior. Still, because I was doing more and more elder-care planning, I opened the Estate and Elder Planning Center a year earlier in Franklin, Tennessee. By the end of that year, the volume of people asking for help with their elder-care planning had become so great that I focused on their issues for the next two years.

As an investment advisor, my job is to help people mindfully grow their money, make sure their risk tolerance is well-heeded, and plan carefully to ensure they have the right portfolio mix and income streams. My goal always is for my clients to have a great retirement.

By 2012, I had decided to turn my focus back to helping people retire successfully. But after what I had seen in the trenches of elder-care planning,

WHEN RETIREMENT GOES BAD—LIFE SUCKS

I knew every plan had to include something that would provide extra money from outside the portfolio should they need to pay for care not covered by Medicare as they aged.

It was tough when I went back to investment advising, but I made sure that every client we worked with included a plan to handle what I quickly came to call the "ticking time bomb" in pretty much everyone's investment portfolio. It was a defect of massive proportions because I also realized, fairly quickly, that the financial planning and investment advising community—my chosen profession—had been asleep at the wheel. Because when that bomb went off, the portfolio was no longer just "defective," it was decimated, and all the hard work my clients and I did together to preserve their wealth would be wasted.

Pretty much everyone is now aware of the "triple threat" of retirement. This is what happens to your money when you have (1) market losses, combined with (2) income withdrawals, and you have to (3) pay taxes on that money (not to mention inflation). But what about the cost of care? I had witnessed the triple threat turn into a quadruple nightmare. When the cost of care depletes a portfolio, the market losses, income withdrawals, and taxes become so magnified that even the most robust portfolios can be crippled or wiped out.

Those people who all came to see me years before had watched tens of thousands of dollars flow out of their accounts for care. They were dealing with this deadly combination of the "triple threat" and rising care costs. And it wasn't just a mom issue or a dad issue. It really was a family issue. Someone had to take care of Mom or Dad or Auntie Jill or Johnny, the old guy who lived next door and was a confirmed bachelor. Someone had to pay for it with either human or financial capital, and usually both.

By the way, Medicare doesn't pay for the everyday stuff—the help getting out of bed, eating, getting dressed for the day, going to the bathroom, brushing teeth, and getting back into bed at the end of the day. The only way Medicaid pays a dime is if you don't have any money left to handle the cost and you need to put your loved one in a Medicaid skilled nursing home. That's the end result of the dreaded Medicaid spend-down.

Introduction—Finding the Right Solution

So when you add "cost of care" to the triple threat, it becomes the quadruple nightmare.

But how could a family handle this?

I first started working with traditional long term care insurance. This is the "go-to" for pretty much everyone. But that solution, while sometimes workable, inherently has two major problems that most people don't like, and neither do I. It is a "use it or lose it" proposition, and the price is never locked in. Because of that, insurance carriers were handing out CRAZY premium increases. Those people who were insured had to pay a lot more for the same benefits, and new policies were stripped of several advantages, like the lifetime payout option.

As a guy who thought in terms of the roles that each piece of a client's plan would play in their retirement success, I wanted to find a solution that would allow us to allocate a portion of someone's nest egg to produce more of a win-win than what I was seeing in traditional long term-care insurance.

I guess I could say that the win-win I was looking for found me. Once I found the optimum solution, I began to include it in all the plans I was building to help clients transition into retirement, and they loved it. They had no idea solutions like these existed.

I thought, "Hey, we should build a class to show people what's really going on in this industry and why this solution is really the best one. It will be great!"

It went over like a proverbial lead balloon. People didn't show up. I had failed to realize how much the public simply didn't want to talk about it back then. Ten years ago, most people could only think of traditional long term care insurance and nursing homes when they saw this topic. Even more than today, people were used to being reactive, meaning they waited until the problem was practically insurmountable before they decided to do something about it. That's how this long-term care problem had been handled for decades. But when it comes to paying for care, it's almost always too late when you are reactive.

This is why investment advisors aren't aware of what they can do to help their clients with this issue. Insurance and annuity agents often turn a blind eye because anytime anyone even hints at "longevity planning" or "long-term care," everyone immediately thinks of traditional long term care insurance. Although the tide has been changing gradually, for some of them, it is still the most dreaded conversation they have with a client.

Compared to what people **should** know, this solution is still hidden.

But the impetus that made me create that first class for people never left me. I have a duty to share what I know with the world. Hence, *When Retirement Goes Bad—Life Sucks: The Hidden Defect in Your Retirement Portfolio that Everyone Wants to Ignore*.

We live in a time that everyone knew was coming: all the baby boomers are now birthday-ing themselves into their golden years. But that's actually only half the story. One of my favorite books, *The Longevity Economy*, is very clear. The other half is the ever-lowering birth rate. More and more people live into their late eighties and nineties, but we're not getting the corresponding increase in the workforce. It's a blessing on one hand and a national problem on the other because neither this generation nor this country is prepared financially. And it's not going to get better unless families take matters into their own hands and plan ahead.

The government isn't going to fix it. The truth is, Medicare is taking care of less and less as the cost of care goes up and up. So the only answer is to take care of you and yours *now*.

I call the solution I found the LCAP—*Longevity Care Allocation Planning*. It is proactive, meaning you aren't waiting until you need it to get it. It cures the defective portfolio syndrome that I saw plague pretty much everyone's portfolio. You put it in place long before you feel your joints starting to creak, you can't dress yourself, and your short-term memory is getting spotty, at best.

It has also proven itself to truly be a win-win over the past decade. You have it if you need it; it's not wasted if you don't. In other words, you can grow a leveraged pool of money specifically for your care in your later years, and your heirs get the money if you don't use it. But it's not traditional long term care insurance.

Curious? Read on.

1

Think This Can't Happen to You?

MY MOM STARED AT THE PHONE IN DISBELIEF. SHE KNEW that if she didn't act in a split second, good people, people she loved, people she'd lived by for years, could die.

She called me as soon as she hung up the phone with Jim.

"Kerry, Jim has a gun. He says, 'I'm going to take care of the situation with Diane.'"

I can still hear my mom's voice shaking. She was trying not to cry, but not doing a very good job.

"Mom, take a deep breath. You need to call the police," I tell her as quickly and as calmly as I could.

She called, and in no time, there were three police cars at her neighbor's house and one parked in front of the tree at her house. They wanted to know what had happened. She told them, and that's when they started calling on their megaphones for Jim to exit the house.

The police and my mother waited a long time. The police kept calling Jim, trying to get him to come to the door. They had their guns drawn.

Jim didn't come to the door right away, not because he was hiding or because he was aware that he had done something wrong. Mom swears that it's because he didn't have his hearing aids on because he hardly ever wore them in the house.

When Jim finally spotted the police, he called my mom, Jean, on the phone. "Jean, you can call off the police."

She was adamant. "No, Jim, I cannot. They have been trying to get you to the front door for the last twenty minutes. Open the door, and make sure they know you don't have a gun in your hands."

Jim said to my mom, "I need you to come over here."

Mom was thinking to herself, *"There is no way in heck I'm going over to that house. He's not in his right mind."*

And he really wasn't. Jim had spent his working years managing his territory for a top greeting-card company. He would go to drug stores, mom and pop shops, anywhere that had a greeting-card section. He would restock cards, make new friends, and let people know they were important. He also was a very active volunteer with Gideons International—the non-profit organization that puts Bibles into hotel rooms. Jim pulling a gun on his wife? That's not the person I knew as my childhood neighbor, but it was someone my mom was very uncertain about at that point.

Jim finally came to the door. The police entered. The next thing my mom knew, an ambulance arrived, the police confiscated Jim's guns, and the EMTs were bringing Jim out on a stretcher.

Jim hollered to her as he was leaving, "I need help."

That may seem like an obvious statement, but this wasn't someone who *ever* made himself that vulnerable. Jim *always* had the answer, and it was *always* right. According to him.

As soon as Jim was in the ambulance, my mom rushed over to check on Diane.

A deputy was by her side, questioning her.

"Did he hit you?" the deputy asked Diane.

"Hell yes, he slapped me," was her angry reply.

"Did he threaten you?" was the next question.

"Well, if I didn't get my ass off that toilet, then 'that would be it.' That's what he told me."

Mom told me later that she was afraid of what she would find when she went over to Diane and Jim's house. "She was okay, thank God, but she was badly shaken."

Of course she was.

Diane, the wife, has dementia. Right before this all happened, Diane had suffered a mild stroke. After her hospital stay, she had yet another stint in a rehab center. She had been there a few times prior, and each time she came home, there would be something new to deal with. This time, she picked up one habit in particular that caused ***a lot*** of stress for her husband. We also found out later that Jim was in the first stages of age-onset dementia, possibly Alzheimer's, so he no longer had the patience to deal with anything out of the ordinary.

The habit Diane picked up was definitely out of the ordinary. She would sit on the toilet for around two hours. No matter what Jim did, she wouldn't get up and come out of the bathroom. We told him that it would require the patience of Job to deal with this. Jim insisted that he could take care of Diane. He reminded us all that they were on a fixed income and couldn't afford to send her into a memory-care facility.

Sure enough, it didn't take but a couple of weeks for Jim to snap. That's when he pulled one of his guns on Diane and ended up spending weeks in jail. He had *no* idea what had happened, and he certainly didn't think he had done anything wrong.

I wish I could say that I had made up at least some of this story. But it's all true, taken verbatim from my mom.

Hitting the Danger Zone

Jim and Diane hit what we call the danger zone. It's where the level of care she needed didn't match the level she was getting. In this case, her care was entirely dependent on what Jim was actually capable of providing. All manner of bad things can happen to an entire family in the danger zone.

What happened next was awful. Jim went to jail, then to trial. Come to find out, he had slapped Diane hard enough to give her a nasty bruise that showed up a day later. My mom was called over by the physical therapist and had to tell her what happened. They called the police again. The sheriff was very helpful, but he was adamant. Not only had he pulled a gun on her, but Jim had hit his wife. It would be for the court to decide ultimately, but Jim was charged with assault with a deadly weapon and domestic violence. He had to go to jail. It didn't matter that he was old—ninety-three at the time.

When he left the courthouse, he thought he was going home. But instead, he was carted back to jail, and the only way that he could come home was if Diane was not in the house.

The Problem Compounds

A decade prior to Jim pulling a gun on Diane, I met with them. I showed them a way to allocate their money so that if one or both of them ever needed help at home, had to go to assisted living, or needed any kind of elder care, they would have a guaranteed source of funds that would help extend their fixed income. They would, hopefully, not feel stuck.

Diane was interested. Jim thanked me very much for my time but reminded me, for the umpteenth time, that they were on a "fixed income." He didn't have the available funds. What he meant by "fixed income" is that he depended on his stock dividends as his income. He thought that if he re-allocated some of his money held in stocks to longevity planning, his income would decrease. His thinking was understandable but included some big blind spots. At the time, his net savings was over a million dollars. It didn't matter to him that he had enough on which to plan for a future in which it was pretty certain *something* would happen. All he could see was what was in his portfolio, and he worried constantly about it.

"Besides," he said in justification of his decision not to act, "I have planned out the next fifteen to twenty years of our lives. We have everything covered."

I have often seen this attitude and know that life can never be neatly tied into a fifteen- to twenty-year bow. Almost always, something will make it all unravel–maybe a little, most likely a lot.

Even though I repeated it a number of times, Jim wouldn't listen to what I had to say. "A little preparation goes a long way to making things turn out better if something happens. If it doesn't, then nothing is lost. So it's a win-win."

Fast forward. If Jim would have had a pot of money put away on the side, he and Diane would have had enough to bring help into their home or move her into memory care when she needed to go— not when Jim thought it was time or when the courts mandated it. And there's a good chance that he would still be living in his house.

Instead, when Diane's mental health started failing, which led to her physical health going south, they had to stay in their house with no help. By the time Jim pulled a gun on his wife, their portfolio had dwindled to roughly six hundred thousand. Remember, Jim had picked stocks that had dividends that were supposed to support them for the rest of their lives. But because dividends had been dropping over the long term, and because of the financial decisions Jim had made a decade earlier, he was in a classic "catch-22." This is where whatever way you choose to handle a situation, it will end badly.

Aging demands care. It must be given whether you're ready to pay for it—or not. And it will drain resources—human, financial, or both.

When Jim was carted off to jail, he was very humble. He told the deputies that arrested him to "take care of Diane. Get her to wherever she needs to go." It's unfortunate how quickly perspectives change once the storm hits.

What followed was an arduous series of weeks where Jim went to jail, got out, but he couldn't go home yet because Diane was there, so he had to stay in a hotel room for about a month (which wasn't cheap, and this depleted Jim's savings at a rate that few can comprehend).

As soon as my mom got Diane safely into a memory-care community, Jim returned home.

"That's when the fun started," Mom says, ironically.

Jim would call Mom daily. He insisted that he didn't have any intention of shooting his wife. "I didn't hurt her," Jim would tell my mom, who knew that wasn't true.

Soon, his calls became more menacing. He'd tell my mom, "I just want you to know, this is all your fault, what I went through."

My mom was firm. "No, Jim, I didn't hold a gun to Diane, and I didn't slap her."

Mom said to me a few months later, "He completely turned against me." Jim called my mom and told her that he didn't want her to call Diane or see her anymore.

Mom shot back, "You know what, Jim, when I hear from Diane, then I'll stop."

The next day, Jim called, "You know, I was teasing you, Jean. You can see Diane any time you want."

But then it got downright crazy. As dementia progresses, hallucinations start. Jim called my mom. "Jean, people are breaking into my house. They're coming in, breaking things up. You're the one who gave keys to everyone."

Jean told him, "Jim, I gave you back every key I had."

But being a good neighbor, my mom went over with the person who had power of attorney. They found everything was okay, but Jim needed some help. They hired a caretaker who charged $18 an hour. Jim said to the woman, "I'll pay you for three days."

The person lasted only a few weeks because Jim started accusing her of taking his money. "Jean, someone has stolen $5,000 out of my safe. I believe that the woman you brought in to help stole it."

Mom told him that was a lie. So Jim asked her to get pizza. My mom did. They were standing on either side of the fence. Mom was handing Jim his half when he said, "I feel sorry for you, Jean. You stole $25,000 from my house."

"Jim, I haven't been in your house," was all she said.

For over fifty years, Jim and Diane were my mom and dad's neighbors. They were really good friends. But Mom had to finally stop answering the phone.

The person who oversaw Jim and Diane's finances (it wasn't my mom) was able to move Jim into the memory-care community with Diane. That lasted all of three months. He got verbally abusive with Diane, and he had to move to a different facility. Remember, this is the guy who didn't want to do anything different with his money. He thought he could take care of his wife at home because he didn't think that he could afford *one* retirement facility. Now, his costs had doubled.

As we delved deeper into this conflagration of a mess, Mom let out more of the story. It turns out that Jim always had a temper. It would flare up when he and Diane were first married. He learned how to control it, but once dementia started—as is often the case—his temper got worse and worse.

"He slowly changed. No one was allowed to go into the house," my mom told me in confidence sometime later. "Diane was forbidden to say anything," and since they didn't have any kids, no one was the wiser.

Once Jim left, they had to auction off the house. I remember walking into their home right before it went on the auction block and thinking, "This must be what the Rapture would look like." It was like Jim and Diane had vanished. The house was filled with their stuff—clothes, furniture, a lifetime of memories tucked into various corners. Nothing had been touched. They were supposed to take their personal stuff, but it never really happened because they were both in various stages of dementia. The estate sale and the auction happened on the same day. It was the saddest thing I had ever seen.

The story continues to this day. They are both still alive, a fact which kind of amazes me. Jim is hemorrhaging money. My mom has good visits with Diane once a month or so. The last time I asked Mom, she told me that a friend of theirs takes them out for pizza. Diane starts hugging on Jim and telling him, "You look just like my husband."

Everything went wrong ... but it didn't have to

When you spend years, literally, helping family after family with distraught adult children, wives, husbands, or whomever it is that is taking care of an elderly family member who can no longer live on their own, you learn that the story I just told, while extreme, isn't on the crazy end of the spectrum.

WHEN RETIREMENT GOES BAD—LIFE SUCKS

No matter what age or how much money they have made over the years, people will let the pressure of not knowing, not looking at what needs to be done, build. And build. And build.

I know. While I was working with the Estate and Elder Planning Center, **over seven hundred** families came seeking help. I saw that pressure in the eyes of every one of those seven hundred husbands, wives, and grown-up kids who needed to help their spouses, parents, aunts, uncles, nieces, nephews, and concerned friends. It didn't matter who, because the "what" was the same. They came because they didn't know what else to do. They were desperate. They themselves or their loved one was aging, and they had been sticker-shocked by the price of care and assistance, whether in-home or assisted living.

When they saw that, oftentimes, the care their loved one needed would double or triple their monthly expenses, they knew their nest egg would only last a third, or maybe if they were lucky, half as long. That led to that moment of, "Oh crap, she still has many years left to live, and this is going to suck the money right down to zero. Or worse."

It didn't matter if they had $80,000 or $8,000,000. Like Jim, they had decided early on not to spend the money or energy on the preparation that they needed to. They chose not to secure the comfort and care for the ones they loved. They held onto their money with a death grip, living in denial that this could happen to them. And while they didn't end up in jail like Jim, they suffered.

The high cost of aging does not discriminate based on net-worth level. It costs human and financial resources for everyone. So if you are at least prepared financially, you can focus more on the highest quality of life for everyone and stay out of the danger zone. On the other hand, if you procrastinate and don't do what you know you need to do, then be prepared to suffer the consequences.

Not long after I started doing elder-care planning, I told my beloved, stubborn mom, "We need to sit down and run hypotheticals. I need to walk you through various scenarios we may face with you and Dad so that you can think about it, and I can hear your preferences now, before the storm comes."

This was many years ago and thank goodness my parents let me do some planning for them financially. I didn't want them to be the "cobbler's kids who have no shoes," right? Because they took the time far in advance of needing care, when the time came, we knew where the money would come from to support their potential care scenarios. Because we prepared financially, we could also prepare emotionally and think through some things.

My mom is now mixing her care manager and caregiver roles for my dad. He just turned ninety-two and is dealing with some dementia. He's moving very slow and is more than a bit unsteady. A professional caregiver comes in a few times a week now to help him get a bath, get him dressed, and tidy up his areas. This helps my mom so much. That doesn't mean she didn't wait until her stress and strain built up to a pressure point before letting me turn on the first level of help. But once she did, it was instant relief. Have you ever been an 85-year-old person trying to assist another 92-year-old person? Me neither, so I can only imagine. But I know that when I help, it's exhausting. Now she doesn't know how she would make it without Debbie, the hired caregiver, whom we all refer to as "angel."

Mom is also Diane's medical power of attorney. Everyone is surviving, but I often wonder—at what cost. What's the quality of life? My point is simple; even if you are prepared financially, the human cost still takes a toll.

It's *so* easy to put your head in the sand about all this. But the hard fact is, bodies get old. Aging happens, and *no one*—and I mean not one person—knows with certainty what's going to happen to them when they get old.

We can guess. We can use previous experience, statistics, or science, to help with that guessing game. For example, because your dad died of a heart attack at a relatively young age, the chances of you having the same thing happen to you could be higher, especially if you focus on that. But are you 100 percent certain of it?

The scenarios are endless. But every person who sat in my office, except for a very few that had prepared, all had this in common: they wished they had taken steps to prepare years before.

Sometimes I could help them. Sometimes I had to watch them leave, devastated.

WHEN RETIREMENT GOES BAD—LIFE SUCKS

How long do you plan on being healthy in retirement? What steps are you now taking to stay healthy?

Are you 100 percent exposed to the high cost of aging?

As I watched what happened to Jim and Diane, I remembered the vow I had taken with myself years earlier: I would help anyone I could to not ever know the agony of being held hostage by the high cost of aging without the relief of knowing ahead of time that resources were ready to keep them out of the danger zone.

When you have choices, you're not stuck. You can plan. You can breathe a little—or a lot. When you don't have choices, you're done. If you are out of money, you're out of choices. You think you can't go on. You do amazingly scary things (need I say it? Like pulling a gun on your wife.)

This is a book about choices. The choices you have as a person who will most likely grow old, who might experience some of the real downsides to aging (and I'm not just talking about the saggy skin in the unmentionable places … and you all know what I'm talking about).

Getting old costs money. You don't want to leave yourself feeling stripped of your dignity and vulnerable regardless of how big or small your nest egg may be.

You've worked hard all your life, planning and saving. Why leave a gap that could wipe out all the progress you've made? Instead, protect the rest of what you have. Reduce the possibility of stepping on a landmine.

Your golden years should be a joyous time, filled with a lot of love shared with the people you care about most. You owe it to them to explore the possibilities.

2

What Really Matters

WOULDN'T IT BE NICE TO BE ABLE TO "DO" LIFE LONGER? What more would you be able to accomplish? With more life, you might be able to have more of your dreams realized. Reach more goals. What does it mean to live a life filled with purpose instead of constantly worrying about how much money you have left?

No one likes talking about money. And who can blame them? Money issues are private. But money issues are often the cause of people getting divorced, for example. Money issues cause strife, upset, and unsettling moments when you realize that you may not have enough to live life the way you want.

This is why, when most people start talking about money, they come preloaded with anxieties, misconceptions, and sometimes all-out fear.

Money also creates the freedom to do things with your time that make memories, handle life better, and empower you to achieve things you've dreamed about.

It's hard to confront the idea of what money is. It means different things to different people. But if all you talk about is money in a vacuum, void of the outcomes in your life you are trying to create, the conversation gets boring and overbearing. You become anxious or even fearful because it's something you think you cannot control.

The goal is to filter every financial decision based on what a potential option will produce with a high degree of confidence to achieve a specific outcome you need for the next stage of your life. It often means different blocks of money doing other jobs toward a collective result. You wouldn't use a paintbrush to drive a nail. Using only a market-driven portfolio for longevity planning is kind of like the same thing.

Jim and Diane experienced this in spades. How they invested their money to get *to* retirement did not serve their needs *in* retirement. In other words, their investments were a great tool to get them to retirement but the wrong tool to support them in retirement without some tweaks. Therefore, their planning failed to do its job.

As I worked with families transitioning from full-time work to retirement over the years, I found that they often kept trying to apply the same strategies to their money going forward into retirement that had gotten them to that point. It's an innocent but dangerous way to approach it. Whether it was the investment mix they were comfortable with or their opinions on various solutions based on an article here or there, their "growth" years leading up to retirement never translated into the "preservation" mode their money needed to transition into once they retired.

One of the worst cases of this I can think of was a woman whose son is a medical doctor. Obviously, he's smart, so she said she needed to follow what he thinks. He was young, working hard, and in "growth" mode. Should she allocate her money just like her son? No. Could he help her evaluate options given to her by a specialist familiar with exactly where she was in life? Maybe. Unfortunately, she did the former and got caught with no money long before she was done living her life.

Changing the Conversation

What if we looked at this money issue in a different way?

What if we changed the conversation to one that's focused on what your life goals are?

To do that, let's first look at what's really important in your life. What makes you want to get out of bed, brings joy to your day, and propels you to live life in a way that makes you happy and fulfilled? We all have a purpose, and sitting on our money isn't it.

But "purpose" is the real discussion we should be having—with each other, with our loved ones, and then with our financial advisor.

This book is obviously about money and how you can protect it from one of the most pervasive "inevitables"—succumbing to the high cost of aging in a way that is not in your favor.

One of the best-kept secrets in the financial industry is that money isn't the issue. It's how you approach life, what perspectives you take on your work, your family, and even your world—that's what's important. At the end of the day, money is the support structure you have in place so that you can *do* all those things you want in your life. Giving it the power of being the primary reason for living doesn't do anyone any good.

The Question You Should Be Asking

Let's refine the questions I asked above to something even simpler: "What do you think about doing when you're done working full-time?"

I've asked many people this question. I've heard the gamut of answers: from golf and travel to being the "best grandma ever." Some people want to go off the grid, start their own sustainable farm co-op or grow flowers to sell at the local street fairs. Some were waiting for their spouse to retire so they could really go after those dreams.

At the end of the day, what you answer is important *to you* because your answer shows that you, like everyone else I've met, have a dream.

Maybe you're in the group with no idea about this weird thing they call retirement. It's hard to dream because you can't even see yourself not working. That's okay. You have some internal work to do because, whether you work until you die or not, there are people that need you and what you have to offer. Maybe it's time you put some thought into what you will be doing with all those hours when you're not working anymore.

Your dreams and your purposes are what should take front and center in any discussion of money because they come first. The fact that money fuels the dream of becoming real is secondary. If you don't have the dream, then your discussions about money and how to save it, grow it, and spend it become just another overbearing, frightening conversation about money.

I've talked to many people who feel like their lives are out of control. One group has plenty of money. Cash flow is great, and they have no debt, but they still feel like life is out of control. The other group spends too much; they are in debt up to their eyeballs, wondering how they got there. What both groups often have in common is not knowing how they're going to handle their finances when they get older and need help.

How do you make your life better?

How can you approach life in a way that makes you feel happy? Or safe? Or fulfilled?

Health and Relationships

I have found that to have a good conversation about money requires having a heartfelt conversation about the two other important aspects of what I call "dream support": health and relationships.

I always start the conversation with this: "Think about the next several years. What do you think about doing?"

That's when I hear the stuff that many people want to do in retirement: travel, volunteer, and spend time with the grandkids. In other words, your dreams.

Well, here's the truth of the matter. You can't do all that you want to in retirement if you're not healthy. And most of the time, people want to do all those things with the people they love. That's the relationship part.

So let's break this down.

Health

You want to eat well, exercise, and drink water instead of soda pop, right? Why? Because if you're not healthy, you make my job harder as a financial advisor. It's my job to find the money that's going to pay for your care. Of course, dying younger is much cheaper than living a long time. However, last time I checked, I don't think that is the goal of most people.

Seriously, though, if you don't have health, what good is the money? It's hard to tango in Argentina (or at the local YMCA) when your knees aren't up to the task.

But health also has other vital aspects besides just the physical.

Let's take volunteering. It's very beneficial to your physical health because it gets you out of the house. You're moving around. Maybe you're lifting food boxes or helping to decorate a school gym for the annual inner-city Christmas party in your area. That's some excellent exercise.

You're also helping. You're giving your time and talent to create something good for others. Maybe you make a meal for your elderly neighbor and then when you drop it off, you spend some time with her because she's not too mobile anymore. Her smile brightens not just the room but your entire day. You've accomplished something good. You've done your heart "good," and that has everything to do with your mental and emotional health.

If you're depressed, you do not want to move. You don't want to get out of the house. Sure, it's very easy to have your groceries delivered and stay in front of the television binge-watching whatever's streaming. But what kind of life is that?

There are many ways to manifest a healthy life.

Grandkids are full of life, which means they have a lot of energy. They don't want to be around you if you're crabby all the time because you don't feel physically or even emotionally up to the task.

Read books. If you don't like to read or find it hard to follow the print, listen to them. The audible book industry is booming. I personally consume many books every year this way. It's great.

The happiest retirees I've met find ways to blend it all together. They love to garden, so they teach a masterclass on gardening. They figure out how to write a book—or even a blog—on gardening techniques that work for their area. They stay engaged with life based on what they love. This is what retirement, your golden years, whatever you call them, is all about.

Then there's your spiritual health. What that means to you is very personal. Regardless of your faith or church orientation, if your spiritual side isn't straight, it will cause problems in other areas. For example, maybe you need to find a way to forgive that person who offended or hurt you recently or long ago. If you don't, it's going to eat away at you for the rest of your life, clouding your days that could otherwise be much brighter.

Some of the most well-rounded and interesting people I've met are those who don't go to church but have a deep peace spiritually. Protecting that is very important to them. These are spiritually healthy people because they recognize that there is something greater than themselves, something that can't be seen or touched but is still very powerful. Because they are doing well spiritually, they are far healthier physically and emotionally.

I often tell my wife that I'm part life-coach. When you are looking daily at people's hard-earned life savings and building plans to help them spend it, you want to see them really get to enjoy it in retirement.

I love helping people find ways to be their best, healthiest selves because I know that these people have a far better chance to "live long and prosper" (to quote Spock from *Star Trek* if that sounds familiar, but you can't place it.)

Relationships

"No man is an island" is the famous title of a poem by the eighteenth-century poet and playwright John Donne. It's about what happens to people when they are isolated from others.

In order to do well, we need connections to others. These connections are what form our communities, and in those communities, we have relationships.

There are levels of relationships. The first level includes our spouses or our closest friends. These are our confidants, the people we trust most in the world. These are our "besties" or "BFFs." Whatever you call them, you know this to be true: your life would be far less meaningful without them.

Then there are those relationships that include our children, whether biological or not, our offspring, our family. These are the relationships that provide love and support for them and for us as well as pain and stress at times. It gives us a framework of values from which we can look, evaluate, and act in the world. Family members teach each other, serve one another, and share life's joys and sorrows. This is true for parents and their children, but if parents were honest, they also learn a ton from their kids. (Ensio. Café WiFi. October 8, 2021)

While family and our closest friends are vital, other relationships we have in our lives can be equally enriching.

My friend remembers her grandmother going on trips with her neighbor. They both came from Eastern Europe. They were great friends, and while this grandmother had a very large extended family, this neighbor was the person with whom she chose to travel. They took the bus to all sorts of fun places like Disneyland and Mount Rushmore. They always brought back little spoons to commemorate where they had gone and, of course, took a ton of pictures. But probably the best part was the stories they told, not of the places they went but of what they did together on the bus. They had fun, and they loved each other's company.

As we age, these relationships become even more important. The people we see at church, in the grocery store, the young couple who live up the street who just had a baby—they are our lifelines. So not answering the phone when Jim called was one of the hardest things my mom ever had to do. The fifty years of friendship that were vanishing made her sad.

The emotional bond we form with others is important. If it weren't, then when we lose our friends and family, it wouldn't take such a huge emotional toll on everyone involved. As we age, having conversations about your preferences with those closest to you is one way to honor those relationships.

The essence of life runs through our relationships. Without them, why bother? I hope you are beginning to see how health and relationships are the building blocks that partner with time and money to make those dreams come true.

Money

How many times have you heard someone say: "If only I had more money?" I listen to it a lot in my business, and I immediately think *to do what*. Pay bills? Buy organic groceries? Whatever the person feels that they need, I bet that it's not really about the money. They want "more" to take their kids to the movies or putt-putt golfing. Or buy better shoes. Or make sure that their aging mother has whatever she needs. Sometimes when they come to see me for a financial plan, they are apologetic that they don't have more.

I tell them, "It's not about how much you have. It's about the fact that it's never too late to build a plan to reverse engineer from that point forward to best achieve the outcomes you want to experience later."

The money covers the bases. It's there to support whatever you want to do. It helps get things done. While at times it feels like it's right up there with oxygen, it's not the most important of the three elements that I've identified (health, relationships, and money).

Here's a little exercise I'll walk you through just to prove this point. When I talk to people, I give them this chart. I call it the "Life Visual." You'll see the various points that I have been telling you about in it. You can easily draw it out on a piece of paper:

First, look up top, above the word "LIFE," and insert all those things you've been thinking about as I've brought up your dreams, purposes, and activities that make your heart sing.

Those are the things that you are at risk of losing if they aren't properly supported by your health, relationships, and money.

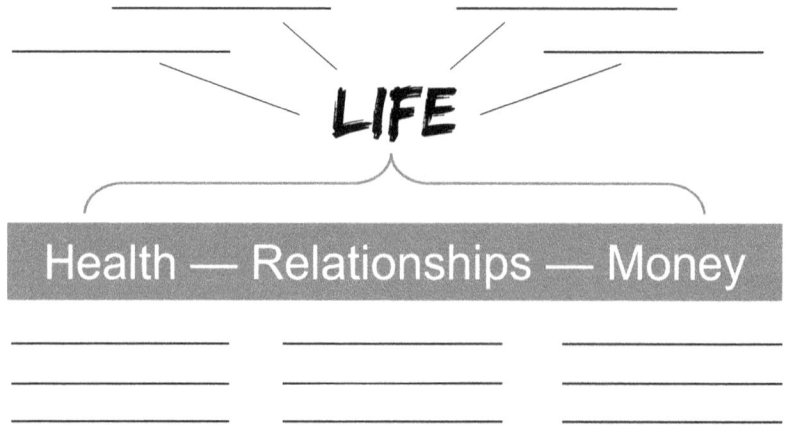

Think about it. If you had to do without one of these three, which one would you choose?:

It wouldn't be health. We need that. Most people I work with have way too much stuff going on, and if their health goes south, well, then it would be very difficult to accomplish their dreams and live out their goals. I think my 85-year-old mom puts more miles on her car than I do on mine. Seriously!

What about relationships? Would you be willing to sacrifice relationships for money? Everyone I've asked gives that question a big, fat NO. Who wants to be the healthy person who has a pile of money but no one to enjoy it with? That's a very lonely person.

Fulfilling dreams and aspirations pretty much always involves other human beings.

This little exercise helps to identify what money is there for. It isn't the primary reason you live. It plays a supporting role. It's there to empower the important stuff. And that's why health, relationships, and money work together to support LIFE.

Think about it. When your relationships struggle, your emotional and mental health also takes a dive. This, in turn, can hurt your physical health—and all that takes a toll on your savings, the money you've worked hard to put away for your later years.

We should filter our money decisions through whether or not that decision has the ability to support everything else we're wanting to do, and that almost always comes down to asking questions based on outcomes needed to accomplish items above the word "LIFE" in the visual.

You can keep your head in the sand about it, or you can face it, deal with it, and move on.

Would You Be Willing to Give Up Money?

But here's the catch. Money may have a supporting role, but without it, we won't be able to get to where we want to go.

So, as the subhead asks, would you be willing to give up your money? Most people I know would also respond with a big, fat NO to that question.

WHEN RETIREMENT GOES BAD—LIFE SUCKS

But you know what? People are giving up money *all the time*. They react to what they've heard on the radio, on television, on the internet, in a magazine, or from their hairdresser and decide that they have to put their money into a fund or a solution because of what they've been told. They make decisions based on what was good for someone else—but not necessarily them. They base their decisions on reactions or greed instead of filtering that through what will empower their dreams. They expect one outcome but something different happens. This causes a potential loss of money. That causes extra stress, and this in turn reduces that person's ability to stay healthy and foster those all-important relationships.

When it comes to the high cost of aging, people are giving up money by ignoring the defect, the missing allocation, in their portfolios.

The Irresponsibility of Wall Street

It's just wrong that Wall Street has not done a better job of helping people prepare for this potential high cost.

Don't get lost in all the pie charts you've had thrown at you over the years in your 401k statements or countless retirement seminars. Make decisions about your money based on what's at the top of your life visual chart—those all-important dreams and goals—instead of simply basing what you do with your money on generalized data or ideas that you've learned, heard, or picked up on the internet.

It's not your job to learn all the details or the ins and outs of every potential financial solution out there. But you can ask lots of "outcome" oriented questions and filter everything the professionals around you are recommending based on how those options will help you achieve your life goals.

Only *you* can tell if something will further your goals and plans and fund your dreams. Be aware, however, that sometimes greed, fear, and good ole confirmation bias may try to undermine you from within. This is one reason why great planning is a team effort with the financial specialist in your life.

(And who would have thought that a financial planner would be talking to you about your money being the least important thing concerning your health and relationships!)

Do You Have Your Money Allocated Correctly?

We live in challenging times. Inflation is skyrocketing as I write this, while interest rates are the lowest they've been in forty years—evil twins to the retiree.

But you know what? You've come too far to get blindsided. If you slice your nest egg into the right pieces as you transition into retirement, you can spend the rest of your life with a lot less worry. One of those pieces can be designated to take care of you if you need care in the future and passed on to your heirs if you never need the extra help.

And here's what's most interesting to most people: If you do this *one* thing, the dollars allocated to that are yours. The money is not gone. It's not disappeared. It's reallocated, meaning that you've put it in something so that the *rest* of what you have can be invested and spent more aggressively.

I've helped many people over the years. I spend days working out comprehensive financial plans that fit the situation my clients are in. I also know that all our hard work—mine and my clients'—could be easily wiped out if we leave a blind spot. I know someone who had a nest egg worth well over a million. He and his wife were planning big things for their retirement. Then his wife's aging mother came to live with them. Before she passed, she had three minor strokes, seeped ever deeper into dementia, and suffered a slew of other minor health problems. They ended up spending $800,000. Where did the money come from? Their retirement savings. The couple is in their late seventies and are still working. I shudder to think what might happen to them in about seven years.

Aging is a family issue. It's not just the person who needs care that can suffer. *Your* health and relationships can be affected, and, in turn, the dreams you have for your life can be demolished.

That's what can happen when the potentially high cost of aging is left sitting in a blind spot, unaddressed.

If you take care of the situation early on, you can take the rest of your nest egg and live your life. Be as safe or as aggressive as you want with your money, because you know that the high cost of aging isn't holding you hostage any longer.

WHEN RETIREMENT GOES BAD—LIFE SUCKS

We will be looking at how this all works and doesn't work together through the next few chapters. You're going to read about four different scenarios. I call them "case in point" pieces. They are composites of people I've met over the years, and the situations are very real—as real as the gun Jim pulled on Diane.

Okay. News flash. In case you haven't gotten it by now, this actually isn't all about you. Sorry. The truth is that the preparation I'm talking about here could be about caring for the people you love, preserving their health if yours goes down, and allowing relationships to thrive instead of being strained. So keep this in mind as you read on.

3

CASE-IN-POINT #1
The Perfect Couple: Tom and Sarah

TOM AND SARAH WERE COLLEGE SWEETHEARTS. THEY graduated from their state university in the early 80s and married shortly thereafter. Tom was an engineer. Sarah was a high-school English teacher. They had managed to help their three kids get through college—and they were glad that expense was over and done with. One kid started his own business, one went into the corporate world, and the youngest daughter was a math whiz who followed in her dad's footsteps but chose civil engineering over structural engineering. Two of the kids were married, and when the grandkids started arriving, Sarah couldn't help herself. She got them everything they wanted.

When they filled out their life visuals, they were very specific. Tom wanted to fish in Alaska, spend time making toys in his workshop for his grandkids, and volunteer at his church doing community outreach. Sarah wanted to join him on his outreach excursions, but she was also looking forward to spending time on her novel—the one that had been sitting neglected for far too long. They both said that spending time with their kids and grandkids was almost a no-brainer.

They walked every day, and they loved using the skills they'd picked up over the years in various cooking classes. They took very good care of themselves physically and were well-rounded mentally. They had a rich spiritual life, and they worked hard to maintain their relationships—with themselves and their kids. But they also know that they stayed together throughout the years because, while it hadn't always been easy, they made a commitment to each other to work around the challenges. They loved each other, so they learned how to appreciate and even complement each other's quirks.

Sarah lost her dad early, and her mom had been having a blast in her assisted living facility. When they moved her into her new home, their youngest daughter said, "Grandma, you're going to love it. It's just like the dorm in college—you get to make new friends and eat in the cafeteria every day."

Her grandmother winked at her favorite and said, "I promise I won't tell your mother about *everything* I do."

Tom's parents were still living in their home, helping each other, and everyone and everything seemed like it was all going to end just like Tom and Sarah had planned.

Fast forward. Tom and Sarah just turned seventy. Tom's mom was the only parent still alive. In her mid-nineties, she was doing well in the assisted living community close to them. Sarah made sure that her mother-in-law had what she needed.

Tom took Sarah to Alaska, and while he fished, she wrote. It was like they were falling in love all over again.

Needless to say, retirement was going along exactly as they planned. Sarah's pension was their base, and they were managing the withdrawals from their IRA savings so that they were not depleting their nest egg too quickly. They were surprised at how much tax they ended up paying. It was more than they originally thought when they started their 401(k) savings plans, but because they had worked through the stock and bond market crashes of the 2000s and had stayed invested, it looked like they were set to live the rest of their lives without having to worry about finances.

3 • The Perfect Couple: Tom and Sarah

Another decade passed. Tom and Sarah were now in their 80s. Their grandkids were in college. Things started getting shaky when Sarah suffered a stroke. Her right side was affected, causing her right foot to drag when she walked. Her speech was impaired, and it was hard for her to concentrate. She could no longer keep up with the housework. Her kids decided that they needed to get in-home healthcare and have physical therapists come in long after her Medicare stopped paying for therapy. It was supposed to be a temporary solution, and while physical therapy was phased out, home health care never completely went away and was paid for out of pocket.

Still, Tom and Sarah managed. They had to be a little more careful about what they could spend. One of the grandkids had wanted to start a business since she was twelve, and Sarah had always promised that she would help, but that was no longer possible in the big way Sarah had always dreamed about. Money was going out the door far faster than she and Tom had ever planned on spending.

Through all of this, Tom was so wonderfully helpful. His love for Sarah showed in all the little ways he worked to make her comfortable. He took over all the cooking duties and kept the house tidy with the help of home healthcare. But there was a problem. At first, no one seemed to notice, but he was continually "misplacing" his car keys. He would mix up his words and forget where he was. The family, including him, would laugh at all his mishaps.

But when it became obvious that Tom had developed a marked disinterest in what was happening to his children and grandchildren, their son put his foot down. "Dad needs to get tested for memory issues." It was devastating, but the kids all agreed. When the tests came back, it wasn't what they feared most. Tom didn't have Alzheimer's, but the dementia that was present was going to get worse, so they had better prepare to put him into memory care sooner rather than later.

This is where things get interesting. Tom and Sarah's three kids had some difficult decisions to make. What should they do with Mom if they put Dad into memory care? Should she stay home while home healthcare is ramped up? Could she go into memory care with her husband or be moved into assisted living? Sarah's mother had thrived in her assisted living facility. Her kids weren't sure Sarah would do as well.

They talked about having Sarah come live with one of them, but no one was able to handle the enormous responsibility of being Sarah's caregiver. To top it off, the eldest, the son who went into business for himself, became more than a little disgruntled at the amount of money they were getting ready to spend.

The perfect couple who had planned and done everything their financial advisor had told them to do, Tom and Sarah suddenly found that their perfectly planned retirement was unraveling, and quickly.

They didn't have a long-term care insurance policy of any kind. Tom and Sarah's financial advisor had gotten a quote for traditional long-term care about a decade prior. Only because they had brought it up to him in an annual review. They turned it down, however, because they felt the cost was too high for the amount of coverage they would get. In their mind, they were still ten feet tall and bulletproof, so it didn't make sense, and they weren't shown the value. Their financial advisor agreed with the decision. "Your assets will take care of any long-term issues." In other words, the financial advisor was saying, "You'll just have to pay for the aging issues out of pocket."

Tom and Sarah spent around $5,000 a month while living in their home. But once Tom went into memory care, their monthly bill would double to $10,000 a month. Sarah was going to need additional care, so it would cost even more.

Now let's look at what could have been different.

What if Tom and Sarah didn't bring in home health care after her stroke? The kids had to come over on the weekends to help. Mom and Dad put on a brave face, so the kids wouldn't know how bad it really was. Instead of their healthy meals prepared with fresh ingredients, Tom and Sarah started eating a lot of hot dogs and frozen dinners. It wasn't to save any money (their grocery bill actually increased). They couldn't cook for themselves anymore, so prepared food was the easiest solution.

3 • The Perfect Couple: Tom and Sarah

Because Tom was becoming less and less able to remember anything, Sarah had to make sure that he took a bath, combed his hair, brushed his teeth, plus a myriad of other things that he needed help with. She was still physically compromised because of the stroke, but she felt that it was her duty to care for her husband. She was becoming increasingly irritable, and the after-effects of her stroke (the walking, talking, and inability to put sentences together) were worsening because she was so tired.

The tension was like a rubber band that stretched tighter and tighter. Finally, Sarah suffered another stroke because the stress was too much. The kids took turns staying with Dad and found out how much care he actually needed. And because this time he couldn't take care of his wife, she went to rehab. When she stopped improving, Medicare stopped paying, as it always does. Once the insurance money ran out, a discharge planner let the family know that their beloved mom and dad were no longer able to take care of themselves. This well-meaning but no-nonsense woman advised them that they either needed to put their parents in the proper facilities or hire home health care for their mom and put their dad into memory care.

What happened was inevitable. First, Tom and Sarah had to start paying for home health care. At forty-four hours a week, that was $60K per year. That was on top of the $60K they were already spending each year just to live. Then when Tom had to go to memory care, the cost of care doubled.

Their nest egg dwindled rapidly. The kids finally convinced Sarah that she needed to go to a place that would be able to help her because that would save money. But unfortunately, she was too infirm to go to assisted living, so she ended up in a skilled nursing home, and for many years, until Tom passed away, they were paying around $120,000.

Tom and Sarah didn't plan for this to happen. Unfortunately, their retirement couldn't cover the heavy load, so their worst fears were realized. Tom wasn't aware enough to know, which was a blessing because the hard fact that they had run out of money would have hastened his demise. Sarah was devastated. She never wanted to be a burden on her adult children, but that's what happened. She finally passed away at 92, but she hadn't been her bright, cheerful self for a long time prior to that. It was hard to watch.

WHEN RETIREMENT GOES BAD—LIFE SUCKS

I found through my work at The Estate and Elder Planning Center that

1. The money people had worked so hard to save never recovered.
2. The hit their portfolio took was far worse than any market downturn.
3. The high cost of aging was apparent even before they took a major hit to their nest egg.
4. The negative impact this had on their family was undeniable.

Even those who seemingly planned for "everything" forgot to set aside a portion of their savings to help them when they needed it the most—when they were aging, infirm, and unable to make up any of the damage financially.

4

The Danger Zone—The Four Lines that Define the High Cost of Aging

YOU'RE SITTING BACK ON THE COUCH WATCHING YOUR favorite show, and before long, that financial commercial comes on with the happy couple riding bikes in the south of France. A friend and mentor of mine, Timothy Takacs, a guru elder-law attorney, has always reacted to this scene with a bit of a chuckle. He's spent much of his career, as I have, helping people with the "alternate ending" to the bike scenario.

I fully encourage you to ride bikes in the south of France—or wherever your fancy takes you while in your "go-go years"—what retirement expert Tom Hegna says are the first five to ten years after you retire when you're still able to travel, dance, and do the things you always wanted to when you retire.

The "alternate ending" is the path that may involve a walker more than a bike in your slow-go (when you're slowing down") or your no-go years (when you're like Sarah and Tom in the later years). In other words, the "alternative" is all-too-often the real ending to most of our stories.

But what happens when you experience this "alternate ending" prematurely? Or worse, what if this "alternate ending" happened unnecessarily?

WHEN RETIREMENT GOES BAD—LIFE SUCKS

As we age, we continue to believe that we are ten feet tall and bulletproof like Tom and Sarah. Over the years in the classes I've done on retirement, we have always done this survey: Take your current age. Then think about how old you actually feel. Subtract the two. I feel about sixteen years younger than I actually am. Most people feel about thirteen years younger. So if you're sixty, you might feel about forty-seven. This is one of the main reasons why it's really hard to think about preparing for those later years when aging gets expensive.

But to show my classes how little time you actually have to take action, I also provided everyone in the class with a tape measure. Inches equaled years. We would have everyone lay out the tape in front of them. They would put their left thumb on their current age. What was to the left of that number represented the life they had lived. Then we would have them put their right thumb on the one-hundred-inch mark. The space in between represented the time that they theoretically had remaining. All kinds of weird sounds came out of those people. I would tell the class, "Let's make sure it's as smooth a ride as possible."

Try it on yourself. My friend's mom, who is 86 and has difficulty doing pretty much everything, thinks that she's in her sixties and is invincible.

You may still be thinking, "but won't I always 'bounce back' from whatever ails me, just like I always have?"

At some point in our aging journey, most of us come face-to-face with the difference between our natural instinct to stay independent (a.k.a. not ask for help) and the level of assistance that we actually need. It's very common for us to be innocently in denial about what's really going on. It's like a blind spot.

This blind spot is what Takacs refers to as the "Danger Zone." This is when the level of care we need is significantly more than what we are actually getting.

The Danger Zone puts us at risk of leapfrogging down the aging path. This is when you need care, but you (and/or your family) don't want to pay for it. So you suffer along until suddenly you need more care than what

4 • The Danger Zone—The Four Lines that Define the High Cost of Aging

you would have needed had you been getting the proper amount of care in the first place.

This kind of leapfrogging in care costs resources of every kind: mental, physical, and financial. When I worked with those seven-hundred-plus families, many had come because they had reached the starting point of having to get care, but they didn't know what to do or how they were going to pay for it.

Because I saw this dynamic repeatedly, I am sharing this with you as a warning. If you plan *proactively* in your 50's or 60's (a novel concept, right?) you can avoid the Danger Zone when the time comes. And that means you and your loved ones have a far greater chance of living a better life.

Of course, most people want to be reactive. They think, "I'll deal with this Danger Zone issue later." But when "later" gets there, it may be too late to do anything except continue to react. That's when things get expensive. And that's why we call this missing allocation in your portfolio the "hidden defect" that everyone wants to ignore.

The Four Lines

Many years ago, Takacs built a simple framework. It has four lines or continuums, if you will, that he calls the Elder Care Journey.

The purpose of these four lines isn't to confuse you or make you feel bad about what you've not done. Rather, Takacs and those who use the four-line continuum simply want you to better understand what's happening at various stages of this Elder Care journey. We don't want you to get caught in the Danger Zone and have to live an alternative ending that you never envisioned.

Here's how it works.

The Functionality line:
This is the first of the four lines.

WHEN RETIREMENT GOES BAD—LIFE SUCKS

As you can see, we start off as healthy, vigorous seniors, and as we age, our level of function goes down. Sometimes this happens slowly or gradually. Sometimes it's event-driven and quick, like having a stroke or falling and breaking an arm or a hip.

The Home-Sweet-Home line:

The second line represents the actual type and level of care needed.

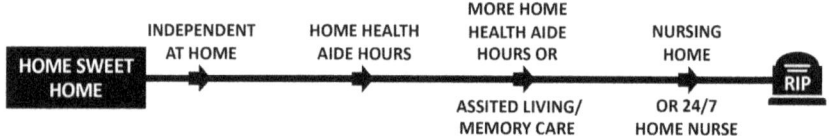

It's a common path that once we raise the white flag and relent to getting care because everybody can't ignore it anymore, we start some home-health hours. But, of course, everyone wants to stay at home for as long as they can, so these home-health hours need to be increased more and more until they force some bigger decisions. Unfortunately, money is often the central factor in those decisions.

The Cost-of-Care line:

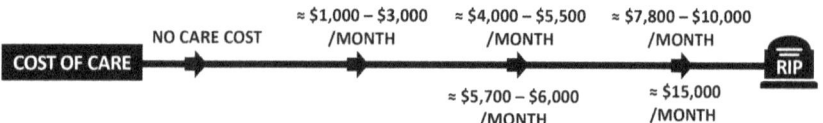

As you can see, the cost of care rapidly increases as you increase the number of hours of home health and the type of care required. We have always observed that home-healthcare prices eventually reach a point where it's cheaper to live in an assisted living facility than to stay in the home. Another observation we made over the years, although I'd like to think it's changing, is that when many people hear the words "assisted living," they still picture a nursing home.

Assisted living is based on a community, not a facility. The "f" word (facility) means "skilled nursing care," which is how the industry refers to nursing homes. We don't use the "f" word to describe "assisted living" because they are normally a bustle of activity that keeps their residents

4 • The Danger Zone—The Four Lines that Define the High Cost of Aging

supplied with all the physical, social, and community involvement they can stand.

I'll never forget Zoey and Paul. They were living at home and had no kids. God had sent an angel named Nicole, their next-door neighbor, to help them. When she first walked into our office on their behalf, she was stressed, and I swear her blood pressure was spiking because her face was red. Although Zoey and Paul had saved over a million dollars, they were living on peanut butter and crackers. It was bad. We built a plan to get them some care, make the money last, and marshal all resources possible to raise their quality of life back to where it should be. Nicole's stress and blood pressure was doing much better after putting a plan in place. Paul eventually passed away, and Zoey continued to live in the house alone, but her homecare costs were soaring, and her morale was plummeting without Paul there.

I'm the guy whose job was to sit in my office with Nicole and Zoey and explain that if Zoey stayed at home with the current homecare spending rate, she would be broke in three years. But if she moved to a nice assisted living not far from her home, she would have the money to stay there as long as she could live. Part of the reason she wouldn't run out of money was that she could sell her house and replenish the assets. It was that big of a difference. Paul and Zoey had no specially designed insurance to pay anything, so all their care had come out of their nest egg.

Of course, Zoey pushed back at first. It's a scary thing to contemplate leaving your home and going to a new place at any age, much less when you're feeling the most vulnerable you've ever felt in your whole life.

After about a month, Zoey came around and was open to the assisted-living idea. She decided that the idea of going broke was even scarier than moving. She made preparations to move to an assisted living community nearby, and then her dog would follow. She loved it so much that she decided not to bring her dog. She moved a few years later to memory care, and then lived for a short time in skilled nursing before she passed.

I share this story because it's a perfect example of how assisted living can be less expensive and better for someone than staying at home when the time is right. Zoey went from being lonely at home to having tons of friends in her new community. As a result, her quality of life went up, not down. Not to mention, she went from peanut butter and crackers to pork chops and gravy.

The Resources line:

This is the fourth and final line in the elder-care journey.

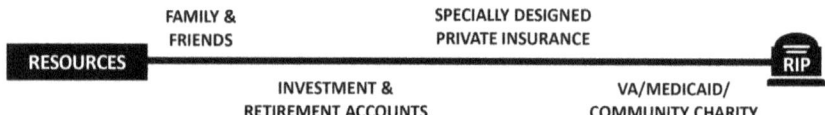

All resources are finite. I witnessed this truth about aging time and again.

"Resources" are not just the money that can run out. When you are the friend or family caregiver and you are giving, and giving, and giving of yourself to care for your friend or loved one, you begin to understand that the depth of what you can give is limited without harming yourself and your family.

After the next case study, I talk about care managing versus caregiving in some depth. Suffice it to say here that caregiving consumes time, health, energy, relationships, and financial resources. The damage to all these resources can be alleviated, if not done away with altogether, if the elder involved had planned earlier and taken some steps to help those around them.

When you have a flow of money available to pay for care, the reservoirs of friends and family who will still help out and express their love do not have to be exhausted. They have more energy and time to be friends, spouses, sons, and daughters. This truly raises the quality of life of the older person first and foremost and everyone else's life around them.

All the money you have saved is a finite resource. This is something everyone should be well-aware of. No one wants to hear that awful sucking sound coming from their investment accounts because they're being bled dry, and it's basically too late to do anything about it.

4 • The Danger Zone—The Four Lines that Define the High Cost of Aging

Now, here are the four lines of the Elder-Care journey all together:

THE ELDER CARE JOURNEY
PHYSICAL and/or COGNITIVE

LEVEL OF FUNCTION
HEALTHY VIGOROUS SENIOR → IMPAIRED MOBILITY / COGNITIVE → CANNOT LIVE ALONE → 24/7 CARE SOME NURSING → RIP

HOME SWEET HOME
INDEPENDENT AT HOME → HOME HEALTH AIDE HOURS → MORE HOME HEALTH AIDE HOURS OR ASSITED LIVING/ MEMORY CARE → NURSING HOME OR 24/7 HOME NURSE → RIP

COST OF CARE
NO CARE COST → ≈ $1,000 – $3,000 /MONTH → ≈ $4,000 – $5,500 /MONTH or ≈ $5,700 – $6,000 /MONTH → ≈ $7,800 – $10,000 /MONTH or ≈ $15,000 /MONTH → RIP

RESOURCES
FAMILY & FRIENDS → INVESTMENT & RETIREMENT ACCOUNTS → SPECIALLY DESIGNED PRIVATE INSURANCE → VA/MEDICAID/ COMMUNITY CHARITY → RIP

WHEN RETIREMENT GOES BAD—LIFE SUCKS

And here's how the Danger Zone works with the four lines.

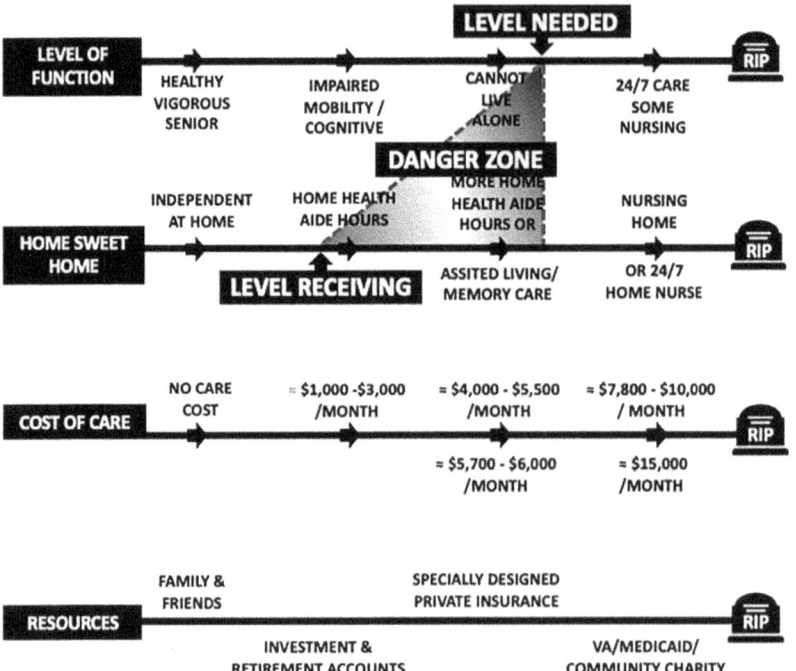

It's an inverted triangle.

1. Start with the level of care actually needed on the Level of Function line.
2. Draw a diagonal line down to the level of care that's actually being given on the Home Sweet Home line.
3. Complete the triangle and fill in the area of the triangle.

That area that's filled in is the Danger Zone.

4 • The Danger Zone—The Four Lines that Define the High Cost of Aging

As I witnessed family after family hit this point, I realized that there were three primary contributing factors:

1. Innocent Denial
2. Money
3. Simple ignorance of options

Innocent Denial: Often when the families sat down and did an honest assessment of their position on the four lines, the elder was usually at least six to twelve months behind in their assessment of where they actually were. But what was worse, the kids were often twelve to twenty-four months behind in understanding the level of care Mom and/or Dad truly needed.

What usually happened was that the elder and the kids finally realized where the elder was actually at on the first line. Whether it was through a medical event happening or Mom or Dad finally hollering "uncle," the family had to start looking for care.

Money: That led to the inevitable sticker shock. Families often check into getting care and then back away because they can't believe how much it costs. Backing away from hiring care when it's first needed leapfrogs and eventually takes its toll later in a much greater way, as I've mentioned previously.

Simple ignorance of options: Caregiving options are rather confusing and not easy to navigate. For example, how much care does your loved one need? Ten hours, fifteen hours, forty hours? Do they need constant supervision, or do they only need help during mealtimes and getting ready for bed? This is very similar to how financial illiteracy leads to fear, stress, and decision paralysis. The caregiving world has its own language. It's not one-size-fits-all or even three-sizes-fits-all, and that can be very intimidating.

Because the family is intimidated and scared of running out of money, they look for ways to avoid paying those large prices for care and start creating all kinds of workarounds, leading to an even larger Danger Zone. Eventually, the Danger Zone takes its toll on the whole family, physically, mentally, and emotionally. The whole situation has just leapfrogged down the elder-care continuum, which results in our loved ones being in worse shape and needing more care faster than they would have if they had just gotten the proper level of support much, much earlier. Need I say it? Much more money is spent unnecessarily as well.

WHEN RETIREMENT GOES BAD—LIFE SUCKS

It comes down to either sticking your head in the sand or facing the inevitable and putting a plan in place.

And this is what I came to realize. People who have a plan in place with a source of funds allocated specifically for this purpose embrace care much sooner and age much better.

After witnessing over seven hundred versions of what you see above, you can understand why I'm so passionate about people preparing early for the high cost of aging. It's the one action that can help protect all the other work and planning that you've done up to this point.

The ultimate goal is to have the
   a. true level of function in alignment with the actual level of care received,
   b. the matching cost of care paid for, and
   c. all of those supported by the right resources.

When all the points on the four lines match up, the chances that those whose lives are touched by that situation will improve exponentially.

Those are the odds I like to see for everyone I help.

5

CASE IN POINT #2
The Widow Wiped Out Physically and Financially

BRADFORD PEAR TREES ONLY BLOOM FOR ABOUT TWO weeks in early March. But, when they do, it is breathtaking.

I was looking out my conference room window as Julia told me her story. I remember thinking that the trees were beautiful, as usual, and they always seemed to offer a ray of hope to any of the hundreds of families that had told me their stories. There's no way I could remember every conversation I had with all those individual people, but I've never forgotten four words that she spoke to me that day.

"Kerry, I'm still tired."

The look on her face, the tone in her voice–it all struck me. Hard. There was no sign of self-pity or even regret as she shared her story with me, just exhaustion and concern. How was she going to survive her later years?

Julia had been referred to me by her assisted living community. They hoped we could unlock a little-known veteran's widow's pension because her husband had been a wartime veteran. We had the honor of helping so many veteran families in this way, and I really hoped that I could help Julia too.

The story she told wasn't unusual. She had cared for her husband for nine years. He had passed away six years prior, so for Julia to say that she was *still* tired made me look at those trees through my window in a way that I had never done. As she related to me about her husband's deep dive into dementia, what, I thought to myself, defines "fleeting" when you lose a lifetime of memories?

Julia was concerned. She had more expenses than income, and her money had been spent down to $70,000. However, it hadn't always been that way.

Julia and Dan had enjoyed an amazing life. After two years in the Air Force, he came back from serving in Korea in 1953, just as Julia was finishing high school. They married. He worked full time while getting his degree in business, and Julia had no shortage of work due to her mad typing and shorthand skills.

Fast forward to the disco '70s. Dan was working his way up in operations at Ingram Barge Company. Yep, they called him "Disco Dan" because he liked to dance, and Julia was in heaven. They had two boys, Robert and Daniel, and Julia had gone back to work once the boys were in school.

Life was great. The roaring '80s were underway. The boys were in college, and Dan had moved up the ladder to become Head of Operations at Ingram. He had a decent pension, but he had also started contributing to a new thing called a 401(k). Julia no longer had to work. Her boys were out of the house, so she started doing what she loved, volunteering at their church and spending time with the wives of Dan's co-workers. They all did "life" together—formed a crochet club, played Bridge. It was great.

Little did they know that it would all change in the next ten years.

In 1995, Julia started noticing that Dan seemed more and more frustrated when he came home from work. He was 62. He was scheduled to retire in three short years; that's when all their hard work planning and saving for their retirement would kick in.

He didn't want to talk about it at first. But the little things made Julie wonder. He stopped wanting to take Julie dancing. In fact, he didn't want

5 • The Widow Wiped Out Physically and Financially

to go anywhere with her. He just wanted to stay home. Julie couldn't hide her frustration and hurt anymore. She sat him down, told him how hurt she was because she loved him, and reminded him that they had found a way to get through the bad times together. This was another "bad time," and she wanted to know what was really going on.

Dan took a deep breath. Hesitated. Took another breath and then finally started talking. She couldn't believe what he told her.

He led the operations team at a company that supplied barges up and down the Mississippi. When he started to "shut down," as she put it, it was because he had been experiencing really weird things with his memory. He would come out of meetings and start to write an email and could not remember the items he had just covered in a staff meeting. He misplaced a file a couple of times, only to find out that it was right where he had filed it. For some reason, he didn't look there. Worst of all, one time he had arrived in the parking lot at work and couldn't remember why he was there. So he sat in his car for an hour before it came to him. These things would happen amid everything else feeling normal. He was concerned that he couldn't hide it much longer.

He also shared with her that he didn't want to go to social activities anymore because there had been times when he had trouble joining conversations or finding the right words for something. Dan was an outgoing guy. He never had a problem being part of the party.

Their two boys were married and had kids of their own, which were a big part of Dan and Julia's lives. One son lived close, and the other was about a five-hour drive away. The boys and their wives had noticed a few things about their dad, but chalked it up to "senior" moments, especially because their mom hadn't said anything.

Now that Julia was in the know, she told him, "I'm going to help you." They had lived their lives with "can do" attitudes. They were determined to find a way to get through this. They even prayed that they could possibly even conquer it. It reaffirmed their love for each other in the most beautiful, selfless way.

They realized that Dan might need to retire early in the next few months, which he did. His pension and his Social Security were reduced a little, but between the two, they could pay their bills and still save a little.

Now that Dan didn't have the pressures of work, he was a lot happier. The doctor told the couple that he believed Dan had early-onset dementia. This was definitely scary to hear. Back then, there was only one medication available. It had mixed reviews because it helped him do a little better on their tests, but it really didn't stop the disease from progressing. The boys took it pretty hard and started making more effort for the families to see each other. They wanted to enjoy the time that their dad had.

Dan and Julia made the best of it. They had their home paid for and had saved about $700,000 in the 401k that Dan had contributed to.

As is most often the case, Dan declined in progressive steps, and with each step, the load on Julia got heavier and heavier. Finally, after a couple of years, she couldn't leave him at the house alone anymore. His frustration had returned and sometimes he would lash out at her. They were in an endless cycle of love, anger, forgiveness, and repeat. Eventually, he got to the point where he didn't want to bathe, and that got really stressful.

Finally, she told her son, who lived locally, that she really needed some help. He and his wife both worked full time and wanted to help, but they didn't know how they could help with all the kids' activities. Julia agreed. They began to look at non-medical home care.

She was referred to a company that a friend had used for her mom and called them. She found out they worked a four-hour minimum at around $17 an hour. (Remember, this was twenty years ago. It's now approximately $30 an hour with the same type of minimums). She figured that if she could get help three days a week, that could make a big difference. That would only be $884 a month. At first, this really made a difference. She loved Dan so much, but while she was still completely devoted to him, the daily grind, even with the help, continued to take its toll on her physically and financially. The $884/ month grew to $1,200, then $2,000, and eventually over $3,000 a month when the care rose to five days a week at eight hours a day. That was over $36,000 a year.

5 • The Widow Wiped Out Physically and Financially

Dan was physically healthy, so no one knew how long he would live. The $700,000 that they had when he retired in 1995 was now down to $500,000. Then something totally unexpected happened. The stock market dropped three years in a row, in 2000, 2001, and 2002. The total drop was about 50 percent.

Julia and Dan's portfolio was in a 60/40 stocks-to-bond investment, so their accounts dropped about 30 percent. It was made even worse because they were having to pull money out to pay the home care company while that was happening. Also, because the money was in an IRA when she needed $3,000 a month to pay for care, she actually had to pull out $3,750 to cover the tax and the care. That means that she was losing $45,000 a year.

Julia found herself by the end of 2003 with a little over $200,000 left. With Dan doing worse and Julia being scared the market would keep going, she pulled all the money out and put it in the bank.

Here's what she was experiencing financially:

	BEGINNING ACCOUNT VALUE	% MARKET LOSS	$ MARKET LOSS	WITHDRAWAL FOR NORMAL INCOME ANNUALLY	WITHDRAWAL FOR CARE COST ANNUALLY	DON'T FORGET TAXES MUST BE PAID	TOTAL WITHDRAWALS + MARKET LOSS	WHAT'S LEFTOVER
Year 1	500,000	-6%	-$30,000	$0	-$30,000	-$9,000	-$69,000	$431,000
Year 2	$431,000	-8%	-$34,480	$0	-$30,000	-$9,000	-$73,480	$357,520
Year 3	$357,520	-14%	-$50,053	$0	-$30,000	-$9,000	-$89,053	$268,467

Around the same time, the family finally made the decision to move Dan into memory care assisted living. It was really nice, and they felt it would be best for everyone's quality of life.

The cost of his apartment in the memory care community was $4,000/month. This meant that Julia had to withdraw $5,000 to cover the taxes and the care. That totaled $60,000 in 2004. By the time Dan passed away by the end of that year, her money was down to about $140,000.

Here was a nine-year journey of a loving wife completely devoted to her husband and his highest quality of life. I've shared the financial toll it demanded, but I don't have room in these pages to share the emotional and physical toll it took on Julia. She would not want us to feel sorry for her. She chose her path willingly, and she pressed forward with dignity and honor. They had made the best of it, having fun with the grandkids when they could, and being grateful for all their blessings.

Having learned so much through their journey with Dan, the family noticed that Julia really needed some help for herself about a year after his passing. So, the high-cost-of-aging cycle started again. A few years after that, she sold her house, and moved into a nice, bright, one-bedroom apartment in an assisted living community not far from her church and her one son.

As I shared earlier, by the time I met Julia around 2010, she was living in that same assisted living, was down to $70,000, and was upside down with her monthly budget.

She may have found herself a few years later out of money and not able to qualify to be in the nursing home. What I mean is this: there are two parts to Medicaid paying for care for you: you have to meet certain criteria financially that most of us are aware of, but you also have to meet certain criteria health-wise. In other words, you must be a certain level of unhealthy.

The Medicaid budget regarding custodial care is heavily weighted towards skilled nursing. There are a few benefits to an assisted living type level, but it's a very small slice of the pie. So if you are out of money but your health hasn't deteriorated enough to qualify for the nursing home, it's a really difficult place to be in. Many folks who go down this path wind up in nursing homes when they absolutely wouldn't if they still had financial resources.

After the veteran's pension came through, about $900 a month, I never saw Julia and her family again. I've always hoped she found a way to live her remaining days with the same dignity that she gave her husband.

6

Be a Care Manager Not a Care Giver

WHAT A WONDERFUL THING IT IS WHEN A PERSON decides to honor someone they love by essentially putting much of their life on hold so that they can care for that person. It is truly an amazing thing because it requires a lot of strength and patience to ensure that this person is cared for with dignity and love. All the great religions of the world talk about the importance of honoring your father and mother, and the Bible, in Ephesians Chapter 6, promises that those who do so will live a "long and good life."

I have had many caregivers tell me that caregiving is truly one of the hardest things they've ever had to do while at the same time, it is also one of the most rewarding. There's nothing in the world that can compare to having your 88-year-old mom look at you, smile the most beautiful, genuine smile, and say "thank you" because she knows how hard you're working to make sure she's well taken care of.

But there can also be a great cost. No matter how much they love the person they've committed to caring for, the caregiver can experience what we call "collateral damage." It's exhausting, as Julia said. The caregiver's health, the other relationships they have in their life—even the important ones—can suffer.

WHEN RETIREMENT GOES BAD—LIFE SUCKS

The whole purpose to being prepared is to help you ensure that you can honor those who love you but do it in a way that doesn't cause so much of that collateral damage.

One of the most important things that I learned from watching those hundreds of families go through the elder-care journey was that the families who had extra resources, or who had set up a third party (like an insurance company) to help them pay for home-health, or have extra care in assisted living or nursing homes were in far better shape than those who didn't.

I witnessed time and again how families stayed healthy and their quality of life remained far more intact when they could walk through the experience of caring for a loved one with extra dollars to pay for additional care. But I also witnessed the opposite, and every time, it broke my heart.

There were constantly three areas of challenges, or "costs," as I learned to call them (and this is where I developed the life visual that you learned about in Chapter 2). But now let's look at those "costs" from the caregiver's perspective:

Physical: when somebody we love and care about is needing the assistance of another person on a regular basis, there's obviously the physical cost. This is literally the daily grind of caring for another person. It never stops. Every morning, they need the same things. Every lunch, afternoon, and night they need the same things, except there are little curve balls and variables and different moods and challenges thrown in there. So the physical wear and tear on caregivers can be enormous.

Emotional: There is an emotional drain when you see someone you love struggling so much. A friend who is taking care of her mom has three sisters who often come to visit. One sister commented on the last visit that it "broke her heart" to see their beloved mother having such a hard time simply moving from the living room to the kitchen so that she could sit at the table and eat dinner. At times, amidst the fatigue, there are moments of sadness or anger, or maybe the caregiver makes mistakes and raises their voice at the person. Or they're tired, so they're not as careful about pulling off the sleeve of their sweater, which hurts the elder, and the caregiver feels awful. For spousal caregivers, there's a lot of loneliness involved because often that older person stops communicating like they used to. Maybe they just don't have the processing capability anymore. They can't follow a movie plot. It's even hard for them to put complete sentences together. The emotional drain on all this is incredibly real.

Combining the emotional with the physical makes for a very tough road for that friend or family caregiver. And this is why about 30 percent of spousal caregivers pass away before the person they're caring for.

Financial: there are several layers to the financial cost of caregiving that people don't want to confront.

First, there's the obvious financial cost of caring for someone. They need a lot of extras, from incontinence protection to handling old, painful joints. Insurance may pay for physical, occupational, and even speech therapy after a major health incident like a fall or a stroke, but only if it's prescribed and only for the time that is prescribed. If the elderly person needs additional care, then it's an out-of-pocket expense. Insurance does not pay for bringing in extra help that can only be provided by a care giver.

Even if the family isn't paying for professional caregiving services, there's still money that has to be spent on extra medical care for the caregiver because their body is breaking down, or they need their own counseling.

The financial costs run the gamut, and the problems begin when a family starts looking for ways to cut costs. It's been my experience over and over that families will pay the least amount they can for the services that are needed—not just for the person receiving care but for the exhausted caregiver who needs some respite. When my friend, who is taking care of her mom, finally got some help, the first thing she had the extra help do was wash her dishes, dust, and sweep her floors. That little extra boost meant the world to my friend. It lightened her load, so she had more patience with her mom.

If the money isn't there, it starts a spiraling effect that's hard to stop. This is how the elder winds up in the Danger Zone, and if the danger isn't handled, that creates the potential for all parties involved to leapfrog faster and further down the care continuum than they would've ever had to go.

There is an alternative path. Individuals and families can get prepared for this by becoming educated and creating a pool of dollars for care if they need it. If the aging person doesn't require care, the pool of dollars becomes an extra benefit for their heirs.

It's all about unlocking a flow of dollars to pay for varying levels of professional care. It's called *Longevity Care Planning* for a reason. It helps the caregiver become a care manager, and that alleviates a lot of the stress of having to do the day-to-day, minute-by-minute caregiving.

The benefits of being a care manager are actually priceless. You know that that person you love so much is being cared for in the way that you want. This creates a far better journey for everyone involved, in all respects: physical, emotional, and financial.

After all the hard work and building your nest egg, you shouldn't have to stare being broke in the eye. This is not about surviving, it's about thriving.

To put it another way: why fall into the pit of the Danger Zone when your loved one who needs care can get it when they need it, and you, as the caregiver, can manage life so much more effectively?

Care managing is about the quality of life for everyone involved. There are too many family caregivers suffering in silence out there.

And here's what it all comes down to: at some point, there is a very good chance that you're going to be the one needing care, and one of your kids or a dear family friend will take on the role of caregiver. Let them be a care manager instead. I want to see you all thrive, and to do that, it requires you to have the foresight and the wisdom to embrace this great idea earlier than later, in your forties or fifties, and definitely by your sixties or seventies.

Build a longevity care plan by allocating some of your finances to an account or contract that creates a leveraged pool of dollars that will be there if you need it. Then, you can turn it on if care is needed without the worry that the money will be lost if care is not needed.

But here's the most important part. Make sure to kiss your mom, dad, husband, or wife, and tell them that you love them—often. Smile with them. Laugh together at the silly things that happen throughout the day, like when they don't quite get what you're saying or call you all sorts of different names because they can't quite remember who you are in that moment.

Because remember, that may be *you* at some point in the future. Give those you love the power to manage your care in the best way possible so that they can kiss you, tell you how much they love you, and laugh and smile with you because you know you didn't cost them too much in the process.

7

CASE IN POINT #3
The High Rollers

TONY AND CAMILLA ARE THE COUPLE THAT LOVES TO spend.

They made $300,000 a year, and their lifestyle matched. They always had the latest home improvements, took the exotic vacations, ate out at the best restaurants, wore the best clothes, had gorgeous jewelry and fancy cars. You name it, they spent it, and for a long time, it really didn't matter. Until it did.

It started when Tony was in his mid-50s. He had done very well as an information technology (IT) executive. He got his B.S. in IT, and it was only a few years later when the dot-com boom hit. He'd always been a smart guy—ambitious and well-liked. He rose through the ranks and made it to VP of Research and Development.

He and his wife, Camilla, lived in Houston. She was forty-eight when this all began. She had one son from a previous marriage and had him young, at twenty. Right after her divorce, she met Tony at a party. They fell in love and knew that they would live happily ever after. She owned a high-end salon. She loved her business because she knew that everything was big in Texas, including hair. She always said that she spent a fortune on her hair, skin, nails, eyelashes, everything—so why not own the place where she got it all done?

They lost a chunk of his portfolio in 2001/2002/2003 and then again in the 2008 crash. For awhile, that made him conservative in his finances. That conservatism flew out the window when the stock market started returning to double digits. They felt like they had done their homework and would be set when they retired. They had their money invested in single stocks and some in ETFs (Exchange-Traded Funds). It all totaled about $2 million, and about 75 percent of that total was in 401(k), pre-tax money. Tony and Camilla knew they couldn't touch those pre-tax dollars until they were 59 ½ without a major penalty, but they weren't too worried about it. They both looked great and felt invincible. Besides, their house was worth $850,000 on a bad day. It had been appraised at around a million at some point, so they knew that if they ever really needed cash, they could always refinance, or, worst case, sell.

Camilla didn't contribute much to the portfolio, but she didn't need to spend much of Tony's income either. Her business netted about $100,000 a year; she spent $120,000. Tony never minded the extras. She always made him look good, and her business didn't get in the way of them living life the way they wanted. She had good managers and front-office people, so she could leave when she wanted.

Tony had to make a lot of business trips, which was great because Camilla and Tony loved to travel. They used the corporate jet, so their trips were always a write-off. When they stayed home, they would spend weekends on a friend's yacht or jet off to wherever on another friend's small plane. Living large was their M.O. They never thought for a moment that they wouldn't just sail (or jet) off into the sunset. On paper, they looked bulletproof—the perfect couple.

But let's take a look at what was underneath the hood. They ate out all the time, and Tony loved his fast food—he had been eating it since he was a teenager. His exercise was all about weight training. No cardio. On the outside, he looked great. He was toned, tanned, and had that million-dollar smile. He missed some of his wellness checks, but when he did make it in to see the "doc," they never found anything amiss.

7 • The High Rollers

Camilla occasionally smoked to handle stress and her weight. She did a LOT of cardio, and her joints, well, they hurt. And as I alluded to above, she was also never afraid to use "modern technology" as the pseudo fountain of youth. (In other words, she pretty much had fake everything.) Because she spent time at the plastic surgeon's office, she considered that served as her health checks, and never thought anything of it.

Right after Tony turned fifty-five, they took a business trip to Indonesia. They were relaxing on the beach with some cocktails when Tony suddenly couldn't breathe. He felt like an elephant was sitting on his chest. Camilla didn't know what to do, so she ran to the bar, screaming at the bartender. He quickly figured it out, called an ambulance, and off they went to the hospital. Fortunately, they were right on the bay of Jakarta, so the hospital they went to was decent, but it was not state-of-the-art, not what they would have had here in the U.S.

Tony's heart attack was pretty severe. The doctor told him he was lucky to be alive, but there was permanent damage. Camilla was beside herself. She thought that if they were in the States, Tony would have the best care, and the diagnosis wouldn't be so severe.

The doctors wouldn't release Tony to travel until he was strong enough. So he and Camilla decided that they would wait for the bypass surgery to be performed in Dallas. The doctor didn't like it, but what could he do? If Tony stayed in Jakarta for the surgery, it would take even longer for them to get home. As it was, they were stuck for two weeks. It was a *long* two weeks. Camilla hardly left Tony's side. She found a channel with classic football games, and because they knew what had happened, Tony could watch them without his blood pressure going too high. Camilla also read to Tony, something they had never done before. They found that they loved it. When they left, they were changed. They knew that they were no longer invincible, but they also knew that they loved each other deeply and that love would see them through whatever life threw at them.

Once they got home, Tony's surgery went well, but they were told that Tony would no longer be able to travel for work. It was too stressful, and the doctor said to him that he might not survive the "next one" if he didn't take the necessary steps to handle the stressful job and all the business travel. Tony took a demotion, stayed state-side, and he and Camilla counted their blessings.

They had good health insurance, so his medical bills were covered, but Camilla discovered that she was not the best nurse. She told him, "Tony, if we keep this up, you're going to have a stroke, and I will have a nervous breakdown." Tony agreed, and they hired some short-term home health care. They got a meal service to bring in healthy meals, and everything seemed to be working out.

It didn't take long for Tony to recover enough to go back to work. He knew that he could live a long, full life on the medications that were now available to patients like himself. The problem was he was bored–really bored at work. On his 58th birthday, he told Camilla, "I think it's time for me to retire. You keep running the salon. We can use our non-IRA, non-qualified money that we saved, so we aren't penalized. Then when I turn 59 ½, we can start taking out the qualified money. We'll be fine."

So that's what they did. They still traveled some for fun because they liked it. Tony tried to change his diet, but truth be told, he never fully gave up his fast food. He'd sneak it when Camilla was out at the salon or with friends having coffee and playing Canasta.

They refinanced the mortgage and did a cash-out because, they reasoned, they were home more, so they needed a pool and a hot tub. It gave Tony something to do, and boy did he keep that pool spotless. It worked out great. When they did the refi, they had $400,000 in equity. They pulled out $100K, which brought their new mortgage to $700k, but it had a lower interest rate, so their payment remained the same. Even with Tony retired, they figured out how they could pay their home off before Camilla had to sell the salon.

Fast forward another five years. Tony was 63. Camilla was 58.

They never sat down and put an income plan in place, so their spending habits stayed the same. Camilla was still spending $120K on her $100K income from the salon. Of course, that was never a problem when Tony was making $300K a year. But since he retired, they were making do on $100K a year, and they spent every penny of what they drew down.

7 • The High Rollers

Their $2 million was now down to $1.5 million. They were good about not incurring penalties, and they were proud of themselves for that. They were also vaguely aware that their good fortune had much to do with the stock market staying bullish. Their invested money was returning well, and they were living off the interest—exactly what their broker told them would happen.

Then disaster really struck. Camilla couldn't shake the pain in her knees and back. She went to the doctor, and, sure enough, she was diagnosed with osteoarthritis. They slowed down even more, but she spent a lot of money on alternative treatments, trying to beat it. Some worked for a while. Others were a total waste.

Another ten years went by. They did what they could to take it easy, and the best part was Tony fell in love with his wife all over again. It was really tough seeing her in so much pain, and he knew that she hated taking the pain killers. But they carried on. They loved spending time with the grandkids. They had two, and they took them to the beach whenever they could. After any trip, however, they basically had to chill for a whole week to recover, and every time they went, recovery seemed to be a little harder and took a little longer.

They were now down to about $1 million, all IRA dollars. So every distribution they took, they had to pay taxes on it. Their income had also decreased. They were only taking about $60,000 in annual distributions. Social Security wasn't much since Tony retired early and Camilla was self-employed. It helped some. His ran around $25,000 per year, and hers was $12,500. Their house had appreciated nicely in value, but they still had the same mortgage payment they got in that last refinance, but it now felt like a huge nut to crack every month.

In order to get out from under that mortgage, Tony did some research on a reverse mortgage and realized that it could be a very good fit for them. He found out that because they had enough equity, the reverse mortgage could just pay off their existing loan, eliminate the monthly mortgage payment, and they would only have to pay the amount borrowed plus the interest whenever they decided to sell the house. To Tony, it seemed like a very fair trade to stop that monthly bill. The interest rate was fair, the house would still appreciate, and when they sold it one day, they would still walk away with quite a bit of cash because they only borrowed 30 percent of its value. The other 70 percent would still keep appreciating and most likely offset the interest charged on the 30 percent borrowed.

This is a good example of the right financial tool being used at the right time, for the right reason, and creating the right outcome.

Finally, they decided that it was time to sell Camilla's business. Tony's heart condition had turned into congestive heart failure, and he was at high risk for a stroke. Camilla's arthritis had degenerated her joints to the point that she had difficulty moving. Unfortunately, the sale of her salon didn't bring in a whole lot of money. She wasn't attentive to it the last several years, and most of the cash flow was from renting the bays to the various aestheticians. She never bothered to try to buy the building. In other words, there wasn't a lot of value there. She tried to sell it, but there were no buyers for basically a name. One of the stylists took over the business for $100K. Camilla basically sold her the name for $50K and the equipment for another $50K, and they agreed that the stylist could make payments over the next three years.

At this point, Tony was starting to get really worried. So he called his broker and asked about traditional long term care insurance. The broker referred him to a long-term care insurance specialist, but after a few questions, the agent quickly figured out that there was no way that either Tony or Camilla would qualify. The agent explained to Tony that he needed to purchase a policy "back in the day" before their current medical problems began. Tony was shocked. His broker had never said *anything* to them about this issue.

When Camilla turned seventy, she fell and broke her hip. No matter how much rehab she did, it never returned to normal. The osteoarthritis had taken too much of a toll. It killed Tony to see Camilla lose her ability to walk around whenever and wherever she wanted. He was with her every day, most of the day, while she was in the hospital and during rehab. But it was there that they learned that hard, ugly lesson about Medicare.

They always kept their good insurance coverage, so Medicare plus their supplement paid for the hospital stay and the surgeries. But after two months in rehab, she wasn't "better." So, like Tom and Sarah in the first story, Tony and Camilla were face-to-face with the social worker, who explained that since Camilla wasn't showing further improvement, the Medicare benefits were stopping. Tony was taken aback. "But Camilla still can't get around without help." The woman was kind and compassionate, but all she could do was hand him a list of home-health companies to call for help.

Tony and Camilla put on their best face, and on the drive home, they celebrated her getting out of that place. Tony called some of the companies on the list but couldn't believe how much they cost. Tony told Camilla, "Well, we'll just have to make it along together like we always have." Camilla vowed to do her very best.

After about the two-week mark, he was exhausted. The house was a wreck, and they were tired of eating the same take-out food every meal because he didn't have the energy to cook. Tony was fighting depression because he had also seen how the pain meds and the hip replacement affected Camilla. The effort it took them both to accomplish just the basic activities required to get through the day was enormous. He had never seen the sparkle in her eyes diminish so quickly.

They had reached the Danger Zone, and they knew it. Tony's doctor strongly advised Tony to bring in some help. He decided that they could afford twelve hours a week. It cost about $1,200 a month, but that was less than what their mortgage payment used to be, so Tony took a deep breath, called, and got some help.

But that was just the beginning. Over the next several years, he gradually paid for more and more care because he knew if he tried to do it himself, it would probably kill him. Where would that leave Camilla? The last thing he wanted to picture in his mind was her in a nursing home. So he realized that even though the cost has kept rising and rising, and his investment accounts kept falling and falling, he decided that paying for non-medical home health care was helping them live a much better quality of life. He could still be there for her emotionally and physically as a loving husband, and he was glad that he could act more in the role of care manager than a full-time caregiver.

WHEN RETIREMENT GOES BAD—LIFE SUCKS

When Tony turned 79, his investment accounts were down to around $500k. He winced every time he drew down $5,000 a month for Camilla's care but only got to use $4,000 of it. The other $1,000 went to pay taxes. Even though they were living frugally on around $40,000 a year plus their Social Security, he knew that the $500K wouldn't last much longer with him taking out $100,000 a year.

Tony also had to stop watching the stock market tickers every day. It was too depressing. When the markets went up, he didn't really see the growth because he was taking so much out. When the market went down, his accounts went down even faster. He felt trapped but had to put it out of his mind as much as possible and hope for the best.

Through all of this, Camilla did her best to stay positive, but it was hard. She was fighting her own battle with cycles of depression, digestive problems, and constant nausea and constipation from the painkillers. She took opioids when she hurt, and that was all the time. But if she tried to stop taking them, she went through withdrawals. So here she was, damned if she took them and damned if she didn't. Her body was tired, her soul was weary, and her spirit was decimated.

One day, she intercepted the mail. It was a quarterly statement from their broker. Their account was down to $350,000. Tony wasn't doing well. He had started drinking again, but they had to talk about it. It was a very tough conversation.

He was 80 at this point. As they discussed their options, Camilla brought up assisted living. A friend of hers who didn't really have any health problems had moved into an assisted living community with her husband, who needed 24/7 care. They had been paying a truckload of money for home health care and realized that they could save a ton and repurpose their income by moving to assisted living.

Tony pushed back at first but was okay with Camilla checking it out.

Her friend picked her up and arranged a tour of The Gardens at Bonbrook. To Camilla's surprise, it wasn't like a nursing home at all. They had studio, one- and two-bedroom apartments. The dining hall was bright and the people for the most part were, well, let's just say not nursing home material. It didn't smell bad and felt fairly modern. After asking her some key questions, the lady there told Camilla that a one-bedroom had a monthly base price of $4,000, with an additional $700 charge for the extra person. Camilla's extra services would cost $500. So, $5,200 a month would get them in.

As Tony and Camilla discussed her findings, they realized that if they sold their house and moved into assisted living, then their monthly income could go towards the $5,200 a month, and they could bank the money left over from the house once they paid off the reverse mortgage. This would put them back at about a million dollars in liquid assets again. They decided it was the smartest thing they could do, so they signed the lease at the assisted living facility and put the house up for sale.

They were going to miss their house and at the same time knew that they couldn't really enjoy it anymore like they once had. It was a real challenge figuring out what few pieces of furniture they would put in their new apartment. Finally, moving day came and they took a deep breath and stepped into this next chapter in their lives.

Disaster Strikes Again

Fast forward three years. They actually loved living at The Gardens. They were eating much better, they had made new friends, and they made sure to partake in the community events. They would sometimes laugh about how they used to dance the night away in South America with all the other salsa dancers, and now they were "dancing to the oldies." But they had to admit, the move had really paid off.

Camilla would meet her friends in the dining room for a little coffee and Scrabble game every Tuesday morning. Then, one Tuesday, Camilla hit the ground as the gals were getting up to walk back to their apartments. She instantly knew what had happened as she felt pain in her left elbow and the opposite hip to the one she broke before.

When Tony and Camilla found out that she was no longer a candidate for a hip replacement because of the deterioration from the osteoarthritis, they were heartbroken. After a week in the hospital, she was transferred to the rehab section of a nearby nursing home. She was there for a month when it became obvious that she was not responding to therapy.

Tony had come to see her almost every day and had noticed her progress stalling. She was so frustrated, and her biggest fear was realized when the social worker came to her room with Tony and the doctor one day for a meeting. As the doctor began to review the facts with her, she could tell where he was going as his voice slowly became like the closed caption that said, "indistinct chatter." She felt a tear roll down her cheek as she realized that she would never be able to join Tony back at the assisted living. Due to certain rules about getting out of the building in case of fire and exceeding their licensure, Camilla's combination of problems didn't allow her to continue living in assisted living with Tony anymore.

He couldn't live in the nursing home, and she couldn't live in The Gardens anymore, so what were they supposed to do? After everyone left, they sat together and had a good cry. When Tony had his heart attack, they had decided that they would always work to find a bright spot whenever they were knocked down in life. They knew that together, they would find a way. But they were no longer going to be "together."

Of course, they picked themselves up the next week and found a skilled nursing facility called Legacy Manor not far at all from The Gardens. Tony brought over as many of Camilla's things as he could. Although it cost more, they wanted a private room.

"You just don't think it can happen to you," Tony would say to the boys at the breakfast table.

What If We Run Out of Money?

Tony walked out of his broker's office with one thought. "What if we actually ran out of money?" He always knew that he would have "enough" ever since he was a teenager. Now, the elephant on his chest sat heavier than ever. The cost of Legacy Manor was $8,400 per month. The Gardens was up to $5,500 a month even with the reduction of Camilla being gone. He realized that it came to $13,900 a month or $166,000 a year when you added the two together. He did the math. With these new care costs and his miscellaneous monthly expenses, the $700,000 they had left would only last for five years at the most.

He couldn't get his brain around that number. Finally, he thought, "I have nothing else to sell except the car and it's not worth much." Then his heart sank, "... and that's if things stay the way they are now. It won't even last that long if I need more care."

That's exactly what happened. Tony, who was now in his mid-eighties, had dementia. It had started many years prior, but now the disease had progressed enough that he could no longer live by himself. Camilla didn't know if it was a blessing or a curse to have him come live with her at Legacy Manor. It was hard to see him deteriorate physically and mentally. He would sometimes get angry at her, but it was never enough to facilitate him moving into another room. Tony passed away a little over a year later, and Camilla cried. The love of her life was gone, but then she realized he had been gone for a while, and she was relieved that he no longer had to suffer.

Camilla's body was certainly ravaged but her mind was still strong. She had made peace with how her life had gone and was a bright spot for the nurses on the floor where she lived at Legacy Manor. She saw how challenging their jobs were and really appreciated them coming to work every day surrounded by so much suffering.

Camilla's son, who lived out of state and came to see her over all those years when he could, was her successor as Power of Attorney for healthcare and finances. He had begun to let her know about six months before the event that the money was about gone.

And then it finally ran out. When her son talked to the business office at the nursing home, he got some good news. Camilla wouldn't have to move from Legacy because they had "Medicaid Beds," and the facility would make sure she could stay there. This is often not the case because many private-pay nursing homes do not take Medicaid. So Camila and her son were both relieved that she wouldn't have to live her last days with the humiliation of smelling stale urine and sitting in a wheelchair parked in front of a droning TV.

WHEN RETIREMENT GOES BAD—LIFE SUCKS

Camilla continued to put on her makeup, including the fake eyelashes (with help), until the very end. She and her nurses would laugh about looking good no matter what. Sometimes they even teased her thin hair into as much of a bouffant as it would go. It was apparent to everyone that Camilla had become a member of the Legacy family, and they, in turn, included their family in her life. It was beautiful.

Two years after they buried Tony, Camilla passed away peacefully in her sleep. The staff shed plenty of affectionate tears because they loved Camilla and all of her crazy stories of her and Tony's adventures back in the day. They knew she had lived life to the fullest and remained true to herself. That inspired them to do the same.

But here's the one thing that they didn't talk about—because they didn't know how. The heart attacks and broken hips—it was a crapshoot whether those would have happened if Tony and Camilla had lived a different lifestyle. What could have saved them so much heartache and stress was if they had built a longevity care allocation plan when they were younger. With that, they may have been able to stay at home, with each other, throughout all the medical issues. Or they could have kept Camilla in rehab longer, which would have allowed her to come home again in far better condition. Or they could have gone to assisted living earlier and had more income, which would have kept Tony's mind more alert. The "or, or, or" scenarios could go on and on.

The bottom line is they didn't *have* to run out of money. And if they didn't run out of money, then how would life have turned out for them?

8

CASE IN POINT #4
Patsy and Her Mom

PATSY GOT THE CALL WHILE SHE WAS AT THE GROCERY store. It was the nurse in charge at her mom's assisted living community. "Your mom has to go to the hospital. She has a major blood clot."

Patsy wasn't surprised. She knew that her mom was having trouble with her legs because she wasn't allowed to roam around like she liked to do. It was mere weeks after the government declared the COVID-19 pandemic, and no one was sure what the virus was or what it would do to a person. The only thing certain was that early reports showed that there would be a high probability of death for any elderly person who caught it. So the assisted living communities and nursing homes shut down. No one was allowed in, and if a resident had to leave, they had to go into strict quarantine when they returned. This meant that they could not leave their rooms. For anything. Period.

"Will my mom be able to go back to her apartment once she's out of the hospital?

"Yes, but there's a strict quarantine in place."

"Tell her I'll come to the hospital and wait in the emergency room."

"I would call the hospital first and find out their restrictions."

"I'll do that, but I'm going to bring her back to my house."

"Can you take care of her?"

"Yes, I always told my mom that she would come to my house when she got sick. I work out of my home, and I'll make sure she gets the care and exercise she needs."

"Who's going to make her favorite egg sandwiches?" The nurse didn't want to see Patsy's mom go.

Patsy, an excellent cook, said, "me."

This was all very concerning. Patsy had heard reports of people going to the hospital, but their families weren't allowed in to see them. Her mom was 85, and while her mind was sharp, her body wasn't doing so well. Before COVID, Patsy would visit her mom at least once a week, take her shopping, out to lunch, or see friends. She continued to see her mom every week after the shutdown, but there was no contact. Her mom would come to the front entrance, and they would wave and blow kisses at each other. Patsy would leave in tears, every time.

She called the hospital. Because she wasn't allowed into the emergency room, she didn't make the trip until she got the call, around 11 p.m., that her mom was being released. She had talked to the doctors throughout the evening. The blood clot wasn't a "deep thrombosis," but it wasn't a minor issue either because it was in the vein next to the main one. Her mom was prescribed some heavy anti-blood clotting medication, which required a shot in the stomach to administer.

Patsy was unfazed. She had no formal nursing training, but her mom was an RN and always said that Patsy would have made the best nurse out of all her kids.

After Patsy brought her mom home, they never looked back. They officially moved Barbara out of the assisted living community within a few months, and Patsy became a full-time caregiver.

Two years before Barbara went to assisted living, she had sold her house—the one that Patsy and her siblings had grown up in, the one Barbara had lived in for sixty years. Barbara's husband, Patsy's dad, had passed away eight years earlier. Barbara said it was time to sell the house because she could no longer care for the yard. But it was more than that. She couldn't drive, so she had the bus come pick her up and take her to the store. In addition, housework was becoming all but impossible to handle. The family had brought in help at various times, but it wasn't enough.

When Barbara came to live with Patsy, it took some adjusting. Patsy had divorced her husband a few years prior, so she didn't have to worry about that dynamic. But Patsy's world basically turned sideways as she had to figure out how to take care of her mom and do her own work. Patsy loved her work. She had put her PhD in English to good use and had become a successful freelance writer and editor. As a result, she was very much in demand. She had always made her own schedule, so she was used to being flexible. But she quickly learned that Mom's needs came first. No matter what, Patsy had to get her up, help her in the bathroom, and get her fed and dressed. Then throughout the day, it was getting her up to go to the bathroom, feed her lunch, go outside for some fresh air, take a walk if it was nice enough, then reversing everything from the morning at dinner through to bedtime. It wasn't overly difficult, but it was the same routine, every day, over and over.

Barbara had developed really bad arthritis in her shoulders a while back, which made things even more difficult. She couldn't be lifted by her shoulders. So Patsy had to figure out how to get her out of her chair, dress her without lifting or pulling her shoulders, all the while handling the pain without a constant stream of ibuprofen because it hurt Barbara's stomach if she took it too many days in a row.

Fortunately, Barbara had her husband's pension and her own Social Security check to help with monthly expenses. The proceeds from the sale of the house supported Barbara in assisted living, and Patsy asked her family if she could be paid a monthly stipend from that pile of cash. They all agreed, as long as it wasn't too much. That was fine—to start. Barbara was still somewhat self-sufficient. She didn't need constant monitoring. Patsy could go about her day without having to do too much extra for her mom.

WHEN RETIREMENT GOES BAD—LIFE SUCKS

It was a wonderful time. Her mom read books and told stories from her past that Patsy had only vaguely known about. One day, Patsy saw that Barbara had found *Charlotte's Web* by E.B. White. They had a grand time talking about the story. Barbara also loved birds, and a hawk family had nested in the neighbor's tree. Patsy would help her mom outside, and Barbara would sit for a long time, watching the birds through her binoculars, praying over the young hatchling as it learned how to fly, then hunt. Eventually, they all left the nest, but that young bird came back one day and poked around Patsy's yard. Hawks never did that, but everyone was convinced that the young bird had come back to thank Barbara for watching over it.

That winter, during Christmas, Barbara had a minor stroke. Patsy didn't know it at the time. They were out walking, and suddenly Barbara couldn't move. Fortunately, the neighbors, Dave and Amy, saw the whole thing. Everyone quickly agreed that the best thing to do was get Barbara home. Dave wanted Patsy to go get her car, but Patsy nixed the idea because it would have been too difficult to get her mom out of the vehicle. So Dave got his wheelbarrow (no kidding). Amy got a blanket, and off they went. Barbara thought it was great fun. She had an excellent sense of adventure and said she always wanted to ride in a wheelbarrow.

That evening, Patsy called the paramedics because her mom was acting odd. They whisked her off to the hospital (and it's no easy feat to get an elderly person who can't be lifted by her shoulders onto a gurney), and that's when they found out she had a stroke. She had difficulty lifting her right foot, and her speech was impaired. The physical therapist, the occupational therapist, and the speech therapist all came in, which helped. Unfortunately, Barbara had another minor stroke about three months later, and the whole entourage was called in again.

Patsy told the hospital that she would take care of her mom's rehab. She did not want her mom to go to a place where Patsy or her siblings couldn't visit or help their mom. But it was now far harder to take care of her. Instead of going outside, Barbara would spend more time indoors, in front of the TV. She didn't want to watch any movies; they were too hard to follow. So instead, she watched the same three channels. As Barbara took over more and more of the living room, Patsy found herself spending her free time in her office, sitting at her computer, watching documentaries and whatever else caught her fancy. Patsy used to spend hours in front of her computer, writing and talking to clients. The irony of it all was that during the workday, it was much harder to sit for any chunk of time because she often had to stop whatever it was she was doing to run upstairs (her office was in the cool basement) and help her mom.

Patsy had to give "props" to her mom. She's a tough one. Patsy used to call her a chihuahua. "Little tiny body. Big, huge spirit." Her mom weighed a hundred pounds wet, but that never stopped her. She was the best jumper on the girls' basketball team, she would often state with a fire in her eyes, and when her second-grade teacher was asked who the toughest kid in his class was, he didn't hesitate. It was Barbara. While she lived with Patsy, she suffered two strokes, a broken arm (because she was the best jumper and she needed some cough drops that were on her bedside table, but she thought they were on her tall-boy dresser), bruised ribs, and then suffered a bout with Bell's Palsy where half of her face fell. Do you know you can't drink out of a straw with half of your mouth paralyzed?

Through it all, Patsy soldiered on. She had several "heart to hearts" with her family about Mom's condition. They all agreed that Patsy needed to be paid more—but it wasn't close to what the family would have had to pay had Barbara needed full-time in-home care or gone back to a nursing home.

Patsy's sisters started worrying that their sister wasn't getting enough self-care. That's when they all decided that Patsy could hire help. So she did, and that was a huge relief. By this time, Barbara needed far more care. Often, she needed help feeding herself because she couldn't lift the fork to her mouth. She could no longer brush her teeth by herself or wash her hands. The list of what needed to be done kept getting longer and longer, and Patsy swore that if she had the know-how, she would invent a way to have an elderly person retract the oxygen hose that was constantly underfoot. (It really was the bane of her existence.) The money from the house sale lasted, but it was a bit of a nail-biter at the end.

But this isn't the reason I'm telling you this story. It's really about Patsy. She loved her mom dearly and often said it was truly an honor to take care of her mother in her last years, no matter how difficult it was. Yes, she had to put her life on hold to a certain extent. She couldn't just leave because she needed to go to the store or have tea with a friend. Dating was out of the question. Anytime Patsy left, it all had to be orchestrated so that her mom was cared for while Patsy met with clients or had a little time for herself.

As Patsy watched her mom decline, she often wondered who would do this for her when her time came. More to the point, how was she going to pay for the care that she would most likely need? Patsy had her house and a portfolio. It was a decent-sized nest egg that Patsy would be able to use, but after seeing how much aging really cost, she didn't think it would be enough.

Come to find out, one of Patsy's specialties was writing articles and editing books on finance, estate planning, retirement, and sound money management. She knew about life insurance, annuities, and assets under management because she got paid to write about them quite frequently. As she watched her mother slowly decline, she knew that she needed to do something more than just hope. Hope for what, she didn't know, but she had to admit that she was one of those who thought "this won't happen to me." That is until she brought her mom home, and her future was staring her in the face every time she had to help her mom walk to the kitchen with her walker, or help her in the bathroom, or tell her mom five times a day the name of her dog or where they lived. (The dog's name was Sherman, and because Barbara had decided she didn't like that name, she never remembered it.)

Patsy also had to admit that while her writing business did well, her mother's monthly stipend was hugely helpful. So she decided she better have a plan in place to replace the money her mother paid her. But her worries went beyond "would she have enough?" Several of the financial advisors that she had written books with had told her over the years that she should get her insurance license. So, being a lifelong learner and liking the idea of helping people get some of the solutions that she had written about, she took the class, passed the test, and became an official agent.

Because of her job as caretaker, she definitely paid attention when they covered the section on long-term care insurance. But she also would admit to anyone that she had only learned enough to be dangerous. She decided that she should get some in place so that she wouldn't have to worry so much about money when her day-to-day living would be hard enough later. Once she decided, she went after it. "I'm going to get the best long-term care policy out there," she thought. She searched. She compared. She wasn't getting any clear answers, so she went back to her agents, and a number of them said, "Oh, you need to talk to Joan Kulowski. She really knows what she's talking about when it comes to long-term care."

That's exactly what she did. Joan came over, and after asking Patsy some questions about her health and financial situation, she told Patsy that she would put something together for her. They met again and Joan showed her the policy that she thought would serve Patsy the best. It had a $4,500 per month benefit that would pay out for three years, and the policy base would grow three percent every year until she needed it. At first, it was going to cost $5,424 per year. Joan shared her reasons for quoting the benefits that she did, and while it all made sense, Patsy was thinking in the back of her mind, "What if I need care for more than three years?"

Patsy bought the insurance policy Joan recommended. She had to admit that even though she knew it would be expensive, she still had some sticker shock going on. But when she would go to a party or a work-related event and the topic of aging came up, she was so glad she had gotten that policy.

Inevitably, others were sharing stories about their parents or friends who had spent so much on care. Patsy would share her mom's story and what she had learned about having some insurance protection. Other than that, she didn't think too much about it. She kept herself very busy writing books on all sorts of subjects, and she continued to hone her skills as a finance writer. She loved those the most because it was her way of learning about the various kinds of financial solutions. Some she liked. Some she didn't care for at all.

Since Patsy was a licensed insurance agent, she got emails all the time about one product or another, but one day there was one that really stood out. It was about long-term care insurance but sounded quite different than what she had purchased. The invite was to a webinar that would teach her about a kind of policy that had all the right benefits if someone needed care but would pay a benefit to the family if they didn't need care.

WHEN RETIREMENT GOES BAD—LIFE SUCKS

She was intrigued, so she registered for the webinar. As she watched, she couldn't believe what she was seeing. None of her advisor friends or Joan had told her about this option. The webinar presenter, Ryan, said that a variety of solutions he utilized didn't have the "use it or lose it" and "price not locked in" aspects of traditional long term care insurance.

The solutions he was recommending always had the goal of solving those two problems with a locked-in cost that would not go up over time, along with a death benefit that would go to family if Patsy never needed care. The benefits of his solutions, like inflation protection, on the other hand sounded very familiar to what she had currently, except he was talking in terms of his policies lasting six years or even for her lifetime. That's when it hit her. She remembered Joan saying that she could and probably would see some price increases over the years, but they *never* talked about money going to her heirs if she died before she needed care.

In the days following the webinar, she couldn't get this other "longevity protection" off her mind. She had a real mix of emotions, like you do when you buy something that you're happy with until you see something that looks like what you got but is so much better. It kind of ruins the first thing you bought.

Patsy was kicking herself for not already knowing about what she had seen on the webinar. Ryan had said that it didn't have one specific name because factors like health, income, assets, and family dynamics determined the best solution for each family. He called the process of finding that "best fit" solution *Longevity Care Allocation Planning* or LCAP for short. He explained to Patsy that it was essentially like any other allocation doing a job in a diversified portfolio, such as large cap value or small cap growth. However, this *"Longevity Care Allocation Planning"* was an allocation in her portfolio whose main job was to protect the rest of the portfolio from being ravaged should Patsy need care. Still, it wouldn't be wasted if she didn't. Ryan was adamant that "the portfolio should pay for its own protection."

Patsy didn't care what it was called; she just knew she wanted to switch. So she contacted Ryan from the webinar and scheduled a conversation. He seemed to understand what she had been through; he had seen it many times before. You could say he was used to people not being aware of *Longevity*

8 • Patsy and Her Mom

Care Allocation Planning or the win-win that it created. As Patsy shared her journey of talking to her advisor friends about this and being referred to Joan, he told Patsy that most of the industry simply still defaulted to only talking about traditional long term care insurance.

After Ryan spent some time understanding Patsy's plan for income later in life, how her health was doing, and the various ways she had saved money for retirement, he scheduled another virtual meeting a week later and shared his findings.

In that meeting, he showed Patsy an option that included all the benefits they had talked about on the webinar. There was no chance the LCAP she qualified for could go up in cost later. It would pay benefits for several years more than her current policy, and if she never needed care, then the money went to her heirs, so it wasn't all wasted. Ryan called it some of the most effective portfolio insurance she could get after Patsy had shared how fast her mom's portfolio was being drained by the high cost of aging.

This was what Patsy had been looking for all along. It was the best way for her to ensure that she had the cash flow she needed when she got older. If she didn't need it, she could leave it to her nieces and nephews. So Patsy dropped the other policy and felt good about how locked in everything was with the new policy.

Because she put this plan in place, her portfolio—the one that she had worked so hard to build—no longer had this horrible defect in it. She knew that she would have an extra source of funds that would flow into her account every month, and if she structured it correctly, it would never run out.

No more worries—and that left Patsy in a much better mood. She enjoyed her mom's company more than she ever thought possible.

Patsy often prayed that her mom would go peacefully. Her prayers were answered when one morning she woke up, and her mom was gone. Patsy prayed that her end would be just as peaceful.

9

The Defective Portfolio Syndrome

JULY 1995. THERE WAS A HORRIBLE HEAT WAVE THAT shocked Chicago. Over seven hundred people died—739 to be exact. Many of them were the elderly poor who couldn't afford air conditioning, or they didn't open their windows because the crime was so bad. (https://en.wikipedia.org/wiki/1995_Chicago_heat_wave.)

It was dreadful. Daily, the papers would count the rising death toll. When it reached over five hundred, I had a friend comment, "You know, it's horrible that so many people are dying. But you know what's worse? Each one of those people came from a family. Each one of them had friends, loved ones, and people who cared about them and for them. The large number kind of hides the fact that we're talking seven hundred-plus *individuals*."

Another friend looked at this woman for a minute and then said, "I didn't know you were such a poet."

Poetry, she would later say, had nothing to do with it.

I know how she felt.

When those seven hundred families came to my office, looking for help, hoping that I could give them something—anything—to help them stave off what they saw was the inevitable march to a Medicaid skilled nursing facility, it about killed me to hear each of their stories.

WHEN RETIREMENT GOES BAD—LIFE SUCKS

The look of despair, the plea in their voice—it didn't really matter if there were ten or seven hundred—each person, each family, each one of those people needed guidance. Each person either needed help finding a way to cover the gaping hole that most of them had in their retirement plan, or they were seeking help for their mom or dad, their neighbor, or their best friend. *Each* of them had a defect in their portfolio that was eating up their nest egg far too fast.

As I have said earlier in the book, many of them I could help. But some of them left, not knowing what they were going to do next. They looked absolutely haunted. It is that look that drives me on today. I don't ever want to see that look again, not even on one more face if I can help it.

I've written this book to help you see that aging isn't something that can be swept into a corner or conveniently left to chance. The ravages of old age will affect us all at some point. I've purposefully kept the statistics out of the equation. I've not paraded in front of you the charts showing what happens to a portfolio that starts out robust, ready to take on the ups and downs of retirement but ends in the agony of having very little left to live on.

I did that on purpose because I wanted you to feel what happens when a husband gets ill, when a wife can't take care of her family, when a mother comes to live with you, and you look at your own situation, wondering what you're going to do when it's your turn.

Going Beyond the Usual

If you've been paying attention, you know that your retirement accounts should have protection when it comes to taxes, inflation, and market risk. As an investment advisor that sits in a fiduciary role, that's standard. I've helped hundreds of people structure their retirement accounts so that their money is safer. I help them understand alternative ways to invest their cash so that the government isn't taking a penny more than they should in taxes. And, of course, hedging against inflation is vital. No matter how good or bad the economy is, inflation is real. It is a threat, and if you don't plan for it, it will negatively affect your retirement accounts.

In other words, it's very real, the idea of "will I have enough?" You want to do your very best to ensure that you have the money you want and need to last throughout your entire life. But what you don't know will hurt that nest egg.

9 • The Defective Portfolio Syndrome

It actually makes me hopping mad that most retirement advisors too often ignore the truth of what's staring their clients in the face twenty, thirty, or even forty years down the road. Why? Well, it's not sexy, for one. This defect in your portfolio can't be handled by putting your money at a little more risk on the front end so that you have "enough" on the back end. Many financial advisors do not view solving this problem as their job, are not confident in how to handle this portfolio defect, and some just simply don't want to lose income on money they are managing to set aside a portion to fix this defect. They instead relegate this vital component of a successful retirement to the scrap heap of "let's hope you'll have enough in your nest egg."

For example, Tom and Sarah's advisor only got them a quote because they had asked about it. It wasn't an area that he explored with every client or was well-educated about. So, when they pushed back on price, he checked the box that it was offered in, and you may remember that he dropped back to his comfort zone of, "Your assets will take care of any long-term issues." He failed to think about the compounding effect of market losses, income withdrawals, taxation, and care costs that they would one day most likely face. This scene is repeated over and over again in financial offices all over the country every day.

Patsy's mom is another perfect example of how the family is out of options later because no planning was done earlier. When she sold her house and had a fairly decent amount of money to work with, Patsy, being the dutiful daughter, talked to a financial advisor. When Patsy asked the guy, "how should Mom pay for increased costs for home care?" the advisor said, "Well, it will just have to be self-funded out of the account." He was right, it was too late for Patsy to build a plan that would have another payor step in and help pay for care. Her family suffered for it, especially Patsy, by sacrificing to make sure Mom was well taken care of.

It's also not easy for a healthy person in their 50s or 60s who feels like they are in their 40s to be proactive. It's not right in front of our faces—unless you are caring for an elder and experiencing first-hand all that I've talked about throughout the book. It's hard to admit that the aging process is going to affect you at some point down the road. But it is.

None of us has power or control over the aging process. The truth is anyone can get Alzheimer's, Parkinson's, bad arthritis, or dementia and could require the assistance of another person on a regular basis either through home health, assisted living, or skilled nursing. Being in denial doesn't make the problem go away. And it makes absolutely no sense to play the "hope and risk" game.

Aging—The Defect in Your Portfolio

So as I said in the Introduction, I've made it my life's work to get people to look at this one fact: **the process of aging can wipe out your entire retirement.** The ravages of aging can happen at any time, hopefully later than sooner, but the harsh reality is that it could happen in your sixties or seventies—or even earlier. It's almost assuredly going to happen in your eighties. It's the biggest expense in your retirement, and if you don't plan for it properly, it can derail your dreams and your lifestyle.

It really doesn't matter who your financial firm is, how your investment portfolio is positioned, if you have "the best" diversification strategy, or where the money is invested. Even the best, most well-diversified portfolio can lose its *entire* value when it's called upon to take care of its owner in their old age. I'm sure you think about the effects of the stock market tanking, your income needs, taxes going up, or inflation going through the roof. What I don't think people ever see coming is the disruption and devastation that occurs in the portfolio when all these things are already happening and then care cost is added to the mix. It compounds into a scenario you almost must see to believe.

Defective portfolio syndrome shows its ugly self when one person needs care. It gets worse if both spouses require care at the same time. The duration of all care can be from a few years to decades, and I've seen retirement savings at all levels go up in smoke.

What Does the Science Say?

Still don't believe me? Let's look at what the science says.

Take the three big blocks illustrated in this section. Each block represents a catastrophe that we should all be insured against:

- home fires
- bad car accident
- aging

9 • The Defective Portfolio Syndrome

Each of these big blocks has a hundred little boxes that represent a hundred families. (If you think, "Wow, this looks like an array that my kids are learning about in mathematics," you're right. Good for you for paying attention!)

The grayed-out boxes represent the probability of how many families out of that hundred on average will experience that particular peril.

Home fires: Statistics show that about three out of a hundred families on average will experience a home fire. It's devastating when it happens, but it's not very common, thank goodness. (www.thezebra.com/resources/research/house-fire-statistics/)

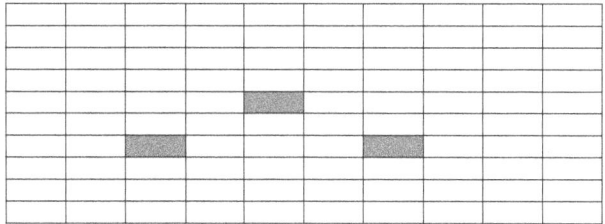

Bad car accident: Statistics show about eighteen out of a hundred, so there are eighteen greyed-out boxes. (www.thrillist.com/cars/nation/how-likely-you-are-to-die-in-a-car-accident-in-every-us-state-the-most-dangerous-roads-in-america).

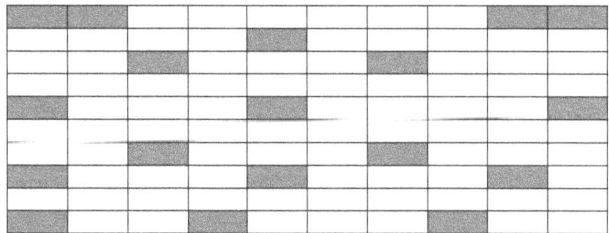

Aging: This shows that about seventy out of a hundred people will experience one or more bad effects from the aging process. (www.cnbc.com/2021/08/26/most-retirees-will-need-long-term-care-these-are-ways-to-pay-for-it-.html#

WHEN RETIREMENT GOES BAD—LIFE SUCKS

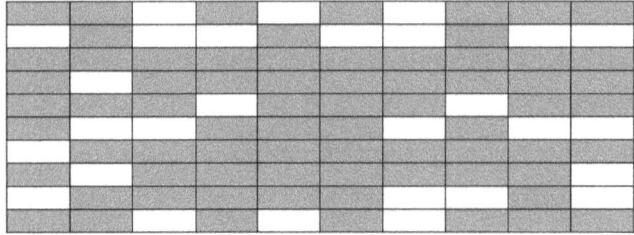

Aging isn't something that happens to "someone else." Unless we meet with an untimely end, we age. Don't misunderstand. Aging is a beautiful thing. The wisdom our elders impart really is priceless. But if we're not prepared, the financial devastation that can come from taking care of ourselves while we get older is like the time bomb exploding. Also, you don't have to be old for this to impact you. When you have to pay for the high-cost of care, then this "time bomb" exposes the huge defect in your portfolio, the one that can completely devour your nest egg.

The Hatfields and the McCoys—A Final Case in Point

So let's just take a moment and look at some numbers, now that you know that there is a very high probability that this "aging" business will happen to you, whether you want it to or not. Remember, the potential cost of care later has the same effect on your portfolio as market losses year after year would have. We have no way of knowing what the market would have done in the ten years preceding the need for care. It could have been up, flat, or down.

First, let's look at what's happening now in most of your portfolios:

9 • The Defective Portfolio Syndrome

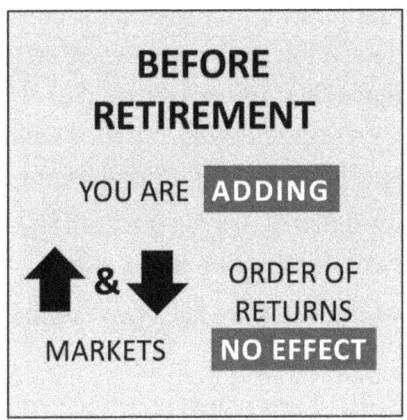

Before retirement, you're adding to your accounts. Your company is adding to your accounts. You're adding in an "up" or "bull" market environment, and then you see those accounts go up and up and up. But you're also adding money into your accounts in stagnant or down markets, buffering those down markets. You can have bad market years early on and good ones late. Or you can have good market returns early and bad ones in the middle or even at the end. As long as you're not taking money out of that account, the order of the returns doesn't matter. The amount of money you have at retirement is the same.

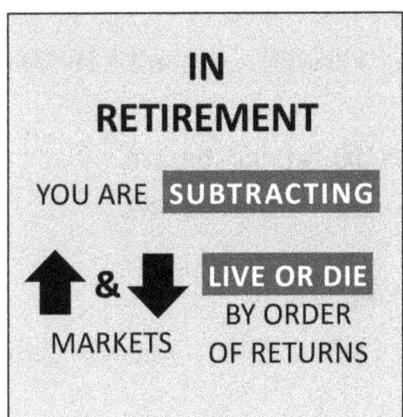

Now, take a look at the "after" retirement side of the equation on the visual.

WHEN RETIREMENT GOES BAD—LIFE SUCKS

Once you get into retirement, what the market does at different stages of your retirement matters. A lot. You're subtracting dollars out of your portfolio in up and down markets. You saved that money for a reason—so you could live on it when you're not working. But because you're not putting any money into the account, you end up living or dying by the order of returns.

The math is actually different. We call this Wall Street's dirty little secret. The fancy term for it is a sequence-of-return risk.

Here's how this works. First, we have two families: the Hatfields and the McCoys.

Each family started at forty-one years of age, each with $100,000 in their accounts.

Over the course of twenty-five years, this is what happens:

BEFORE Retirement

Annual Income Withdrawals: None

Starting Value – AGE 41

Hatfield's = **$100,000**   McCoy's = **$100,000**

Average Annual Return:

Hatfield's = 8%   McCoy's = 8%

Value at Age 65:

Hatfield's = $684,848   McCoy's = $684,848

→ No Difference ←

9 • The Defective Portfolio Syndrome

The Hatfields had bad returns at the beginning. In the illustration below, you see negative 12, negative 21, and negative 14. Then they had great returns right before retirement.

The McCoys had great returns initially: positive 29, positive 18, positive 25, and bad returns at the end. We have simply reversed the order of the returns for the two families over the 25 years.

If you look at the totals, both families retire with the *same* amount. Each account averaged 8 percent over the span of those twenty-five years.

Now let's see what happens after they retire, both at age 66. Both families will take the same amount of income out of these accounts. They *have* to take that amount. That's how they pay their bills, feed their families, and ensure that they keep the roofs over their heads.

Age	Annual Return	Hatfield's (Year-End Value)	Annual Return	McCoy's (Year-End Value)
41	-12%	$87,695	29%	$129,491
42	-21%	$69,426	18%	$152,281
43	-14%	$59,707	25%	$189,590
...	...	...	...	...
62	-6%	$361,226	22%	$1,147,022
63	25%	$449,727	-14%	$986,439
64	18%	$528,878	-21%	$780,941
65	29%	$684,848	-12%	$684,848

$684,848   **$684,848**

WHEN RETIREMENT GOES BAD—LIFE SUCKS

What happens?

AFTER Retirement

Annual Income Withdrawals:
5% of first year value (adjusted thereafter for inflation)

Starting Values – AGE 66

Hatfield's = **$684,848**   McCoy's = **$684,848**

Average Annual Return:

Hatfield's = 8%   McCoy's = 8%

Value at Age 90:

Hatfield's = **$0**   McCoy's = **$2,622,984**

BIG DIFFERENCE

The Hatfields run out of money. Why?

Because they sustained losses early (the first three years), they continued to have to take their income. The accounts never have time to recover. They're done, out of cash, by the age of 82. That is a sequence of return risks showing its ugly head.

On the other hand, the McCoys, end up with $2.6 million. How can that be?

Because they made money—and a lot of it—on the front end.

You might think, "Kerry, you're making this up." I'm not. The stock market tanked in the first three years of the 2000s, and many retirees are experiencing this "dirty little secret" right now.

This problem is a huge deal that only affects people taking money out of their accounts without putting any money back in.

9 • The Defective Portfolio Syndrome

Age	Annual Return	Hatfield's (Year-End Value)	Annual Return	McCoy's (Year-End Value)
66	-12%	$566,337	29%	$852,571
67	-21%	$413,086	18%	$967,355
68	-14%	$318,927	25%	$1,168,029
69	22%	$352,432	-6%	$1,061,698
70	10%	$348,431	15%	$1,177,105
71	4%	$323,772	8%	$1,234,855
72	11%	$318,176	27%	$1,528,614
73	3%	$284,653	-2%	$1,452,871
74	-3%	$232,143	15%	$1,623,066
75	21%	$236,215	19%	$1,886,771
76	17%	$229,644	33%	$2,461,500
77	5%	$194,417	11%	$2,687,327
78	-10%	$126,543	-10%	$2,375,148
79	11%	$90,304	5%	$2,450,746
80	33%	$68,219	17%	$2,808,226
81	19%	$27,833	21%	$3,344,606
➡ 82	15%	$0	-3%	$3,182,338
83	-2%	$0	3%	$3,211,664
84	27%	$0 **$0**	11%	$3,503,440
85	8%	$0	4%	$3,594,592
86		**RUNS OUT** 10%		$3,885,017
87		22%		$4,685,257
88		**OF MONEY** -14%		$3,963,710
89		-21%		$3,070,398
90	29%	$0	-12%	$2,622,984
	8%	$0	8%	$2,622,984

Therefore it gets *much* worse when you add care costs. These costs hit the account like recurring market losses without the market even being down. You're taking out money for income. You have to take out more money to pay for elder care and then more for taxes.

This is why Julia went from $700,000 to $70,000 and why Camilla ended up in a nursing home that Medicaid funds.

Speaking of Medicaid, you might be thinking, "but doesn't Medicare, or Medicaid, or Obamacare pay for some of this?

Health insurance does *not* pay for "custodial care": home health care, assisted living, or private nursing home care. And they never will.

Medicare pays for most of your doctor and hospital visit costs. It will also pay for a short stay in a rehab facility (also called restorative care).

That "short stay," is a hundred days. I've heard it so many times over the years, "Hey, I get a hundred days." Your health insurance pays for about three months' worth of care. That's not a lot of time. There's an even more insidious catch: you don't get a hundred days if you stop improving and you level off. Technically, they can approve additional benefit periods if you will crash when care stops, but it's rare. As we saw with Julia's husband and Camilla after her second broken hip: the care provider in a rehab situation is submitting care plans to Medicare. If they can show that you are improving, Medicare will keep allotting dollars to keep trying to help you get better. But once they must show that you've leveled off, then Medicare's done. And that's where families end up meeting with social workers and discharge planners and get the bad news. These people give the family a list of home health companies and assisted living communities because "You know, your loved one really cannot live alone. They really need support."

Sometimes aging is kind of like a basketball. You drop the ball; it bounces. Left to its own devices, it doesn't bounce as high as when you started. It bounces back lower, lower, and lower. If it has help, then it continues to bounce. No help, and eventually it's done. Dead.

The Crystal Ball Doesn't Exist

Here are three questions I ask anyone who has come to me for help and advice.

1. How long do you plan on staying healthy during retirement?
2. Do you feel you have any control over staying healthy in retirement? (Or another way to look at this question: "is how you plan on aging more of a hereditary thing?")
3. What steps are you currently taking to stay healthy in retirement?

For most people, the answers are

1. I don't know
2. Not really
3. Not as much as I should.

I tell people to drink more water, eat better food, and get some exercise every day.

But none of those suggestions fix the defect in your portfolio.

9 • The Defective Portfolio Syndrome

What is the True Cost of Aging?

We've seen throughout the book that the true cost of aging is multi-faceted and involves human and non-human resources being consumed. Whether it's your mother or you who needs the care, the money has to come from somewhere.

You might be wondering: how much does home health, assisted living, and nursing homes actually cost these days? But, more importantly, how much will it cost in fifteen years or so because that's when you might need it?

There's a really good source online, the Genworth cost-of-care calculator.

It gives you an idea of how much care is actually going to cost around the country, and it's updated every year. You can put any city in the calculator and see the monthly and annual numbers for the cost of care for home health, assisted living, and skilled nursing. You can also see today's numbers and the cost of care in the future. In other words, it adjusts for inflation. As a result, prices can vary quite a bit around the country.

Let's take my town, Nashville, Tennessee.

Right now, the average for 44 hours/week of home health care is $57,002 per year.

Add that number to the amount of dollars you have to take out of your portfolio for living expenses. What happens? Your portfolio loses.

What happens if you go down the road fifteen years? That same amount of care is projected to cost $118,000. That's crazy, right?

What's *that* going to do to your portfolio?

If you choose assisted living, it's a little less. But when you must go to skilled nursing, it's more (like projected to be $200,000 fifteen years from now.)

Don't believe me? Type in this link: https://www.genworth.com/aging-and-you/finances/cost-of-care.html, and plug in your town to see your numbers. Don't forget; it's showing you the average, so half of the care will cost more than the number you see. Be prepared. It's expensive.

The IRS

Oh, and also don't forget, because that portfolio is often funded with pre-tax dollars, the IRS will be there, demanding its share when you take those distributions. It doesn't care if you're taking the money for living expenses or to take care of someone you love. You pay taxes, no matter what. That was the deal you signed when you decided to go the "qualified money" or tax-deferred route to retirement (the 401(k) or 403(b) type of accounts). So even if you are using an after-tax account, you will be taxed on the capital gains when you have to sell shares to get cash to pay for care.

We call it the longevity tax. Here's what it looks like:

THE IRS'S DIRTY LITTLE SECRET

THE LONGEVITY TAX

Care Cost $88,000

Withdrawal $110,000
Due to 20% tax bracket

Let's say that you need $88,000 a year to live and to cover the cost of care for your spouse.

You don't take $88,000 out of your account. You need to draw out $110,000 because you're in a 20 percent tax bracket.

What if taxes go up? It hurts.

But that's the reality. I saw it happen year after year, family after family.

It is possible that you might find some relief within the medical-expense deduction on your tax return. Unfortunately, however, that's a potential deduction easily changed by the government and requires itemizing.

Furthermore, "care expenses" is a large gray area for what's deductible and what's not, and this changes.

The Quadruple Nightmare

Let's bring it all together and really look under the hood of how the key threats to your retirement combine to wipe someone out in an incredibly short time.

Here's what it looks like:

	BEGINNING ACCOUNT VALUE	% MARKET LOSS	$ MARKET LOSS	WITHDRAWAL FOR NORMAL INCOME ANNUALLY	WITHDRAWAL FOR CARE COST ANNUALLY	DON'T FORGET TAXES MUST BE PAID	TOTAL WITHDRAWALS + MARKET LOSS	WHAT'S LEFTOVER
Year 1	1,000,000	-10%	-$100,000	-$40,000	-$88,000	-$30,000	-$258,000	$742,000
Year 2	$742,000	-10%	-$74,200	-$40,000	-$88,000	-$30,000	-$232,200	$509,800
Year 3	$509,800	15%	$76,470	-$40,000	-$88,000	-$30,000	-$81,530	$428,270

- You start with a million dollars
- You have a -10% market loss
- You have income coming out.
- You have care costs coming out.
- You have to pay taxes.
- After the first year of all this happening, you're left with $742,000.

The next year, you have another small market loss and still have to pay income, care costs, and taxes.

This goes on, and even with a 15 percent upmarket the next year, that million dollars is now down to $428,270.

After three years, you may have drawn down your accounts by over half.

Oh, and if you're in Jack and Diane's situation, you're paying double, so double the devastation, quadruple the nightmare.

Statistically, seven out of ten people will experience enough aging issues to need care. If you were told that the Powerball lottery had the same odds, but in a positive way (meaning 70 percent of those who purchased a ticket actually won money), would you run out and buy a ticket? Probably.

So why wouldn't you bet on the odds when you're talking about something not so nice as winning the lottery?

With these four forces at work, you can see how even a multi-million-dollar portfolio can shrink to a fraction of its original amount.

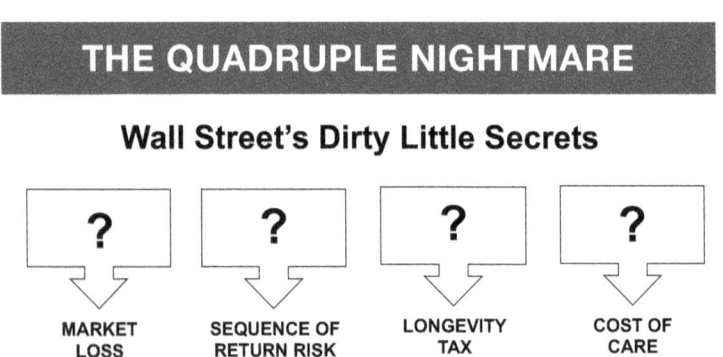

Either you're going to "shuffle off this mortal coil" (to quote Shakespeare's *Hamlet* on dying) from an accident or an illness that will take you quickly, or you're going to get old, spend a lot of money handling the problems of old age, and then eventually pass on.

Given these facts, does it make sense to risk your retirement, not just your money, but your health and your relationships, because you don't want to look ***proactively*** at the available solutions?

A Short History on Traditional Long Term Care Insurance

Let me be very clear about something: I'm not against traditional long term care insurance. It can bring an incredible amount of leverage for the dollars paid in and be the right fit for some families on the lower end of the asset range. The two problems that I've cited are caused by the construction of the policy. In other words, it works like a home or auto policy. You don't normally get any money back if you never use your home or auto policy, right? There are years when your home and auto policies renew, and the cost of insurance is more, right? The premiums cost more because the rates

9 • The Defective Portfolio Syndrome

are based upon the claims experience of the insurance company, and the companies raise them if they need to in order to keep the company strong.

There were a few times when a family would walk into The Estate and Elder Planning Center, and they would find out it was their lucky day. Their parents would have purchased what we call a Cadillac plan back in the late 80s. It would have a lifetime benefit, allow for 5 percent inflation growth every year, and by the time they came to us around 2010, it would pay out about $8,000 a month for each spouse.

The adult son or daughter would look at me and say, in disbelief, "Kerry, you just made my mom and dad rich." After our moment of elation, I would remind them that all I had done was call the company with them and help them understand what they had. Pretty much one for one, these people would immediately go back to the assisted living community where their parents were stuffed into a studio apartment and move them into a two-bedroom with all the extra care that they needed.

But the reality is that this type of product has imploded rate-wise in the last twenty years. As I pointed out in the introduction, more people kept their policies long-term than the companies had planned. That and policy benefits had expanded greatly that wasn't priced in. This is why roughly 85 percent of the insurance companies stopped offering new traditional long-term care policies. They cut their losses because they couldn't stop the internal bleeding.

The few insurance companies that still offered long-term care policies got 18–40 percent more expensive and higher-rate increases approved by their states. It was bad, really bad.

In the last few years, the few carriers left in the traditional long-term care space believe that they have their products priced right now to run for several years without an increase, but smart agents still tell their clients to expect it. A couple of companies have gotten innovative with product design as well, but for the most part, they still all have the two problems I like to avoid: use it or lose it and ever-increasing premiums.

Psychologically, when you apply this home and auto type of policy to long-term care benefits that people already don't want to think about or

89

admit they will probably need, folks feel like they are betting against themselves because they have to need care to see any benefit from the policy at all.

Longevity Care Allocation Planning (LCAP)

I've talked throughout this book about something called *"Longevity Care Allocation Planning"* (LCAP). I didn't just wake up one day and say, "Hey, I'd like to invent something called *Longevity Care Allocation Planning."*

It came about as the result of combining my years as a financial plan builder for the pre-retiree, and the years of elder care planning spent at the table with all of those families in crisis mode. The months of research for solutions that didn't over-insure the risk solved the two biggest reasons I thought why over 90 percent of Americans had not embraced traditional long term-care insurance (the latter is what I've been lamenting throughout the book: the "use it or lose it" proposition and the price is never locked in.

Creating the LCAP drew upon all that past experience, knowledge, and hats I had worn:

- I had to think like an income planner: how a person's retirement income was structured to go with Social Security, how to avoid sequence of return risk, and how care cost would affect it.
- I had to be the best fiduciary/investment advisor: matching the right portfolio to each client and managing the psychological journey of the investor.
- I had to help the client understand that their portfolio needed insuring, so I was also a protection planner: making sure there was enough of their principal protected so the client didn't live in fear of market downturns.
- And I had to be a highly effective elder-care planner: my job was to build efficient cash flow plans to pay for care while helping the money last as long as possible.

My focus was constant and clear: to keep the older person's quality of life as good as possible. During this part of my career, I witnessed how fast people's portfolios were wiped out by the high cost of aging. It became a no-brainer to me that every financial plan should include an LCAP component. It was the most effective portfolio insurance I could show anyone.

9 • The Defective Portfolio Syndrome

As the income planner, I knew that paying for care was really an income problem when that invoice for the home health-care worker or the assisted living came in the mail. So I thought, why not have something that we can turn on to pay that bill right away?

As the investment advisor, I experienced first-hand how much energy and focus was put on squeezing every bit of return from each client's portfolio annually while lowering costs–and rightly so. I realized, however, how quickly all that hard work could vanish due to the cost of aging. I couldn't believe more investment advisors weren't talking about this and concerned about all their years of work being wiped out by aging. As mentioned earlier, most would just take the approach that it wasn't their job and simply refer the curious client to a traditional long-term care specialist. I encourage investment advisors to do a portfolio risk assessment and a portfolio longevity assessment as well.

As the protection planner, I had seen for years that when clients knew they had their bases covered in areas that could create catastrophic failure, they could invest their money more aggressively and stay the course emotionally. This meant that they would be happier and more productive in retirement.

As the elder-care planner, I saw what the aging process of one or two family members did to the whole family. I saw the real goal in my work would be to keep families in control, creating family care managers, not just caregivers, and equipping the family with as many options as possible when the financial call came. Everyone puts on a happy face to the outside world, but I had a front-row seat to the reality of the situation. There is a reason that there was always a box of tissues on my table. This forever stamped into me that an LCAP is for the whole family.

As you think about all of the hats I've worn and how each contributed to the creation of *Longevity Care Allocation Planning*, you may now see why I call this the Defective Portfolio Syndrome.™ A "syndrome" is defined as something predictable, a characteristic pattern of behavior or action that tends to occur under certain circumstances. When your portfolio has this high cost of aging defect, what happens is all-too-predictable, and the family going through the devastation exhibits a characteristic pattern of behavior.

I don't want this for you or any other family that has spent a lifetime working to save money, not just spend it.

Allocation is the Key

Nothing in the financial planning world is ever perfect, just like the people. I simply looked at this planning process just like any other allocation I recommended as I helped clients diversify their portfolios in preparation for retirement.

One thing I love about this allocation: it always comes with some guarantees, unlike putting money in the stock market. I must say that it helps my clients and me both sleep better at night.

An LCAP is there to get the most value from that allocation regardless of the person's or couple's health, income, or assets. The process utilizes a mixture of solutions to accomplish this. It's never "one size fits all." How could it be? Your combination of health, income, and assets is unique to you.

Obviously, the number of dollars allocated to the strategy for each family varies. It needs to be enough to make a difference while also not interfering with income or growth production for the family over their lifetimes. Then, the dollars in that allocation get leveraged up so you aren't paying for care dollar-for-dollar later but basically at a discount. That's how the defect in the portfolio is fixed. You have that payor in the wings to turn on, which means the portfolio doesn't have to do it. Paying for care with tax-free dollars is always an LCAP goal, and one we achieve almost all of the time.

Fortunately, like any great process, it's efficient.

- First, we gather and organize the right information from the client.
- Second, we prepare a "feasibility study" that shows us the right allocation.
- The third and final step is to get the fix in place, and everyone's happy.

Remember, filter any decision you make about your money through the LIFE VISUAL I discussed in chapter 2. You're going for an outcome that will assist the health and relationship components to achieve your life goals you listed above the word LIFE.

An LCAP, as an allocation to fix the defect in your portfolio, is simply a part of the larger, more important picture of keeping your family together in health and happiness as you live out your years together.

The Mayonnaise Jar

I hope by now you get it. The high cost of aging is the hidden defect in your portfolio—as I've said numerous times. It can cost you a lot, and the damage it can do to the health and wellbeing of those who take care of you can be just as detrimental as the monetary havoc it can cause to your nest egg.

There is a solution. It's not "sexy." It's not going to "wow" anyone. Instead, it gives you far more peace of mind than anything else I can think of.

We all want to make as much money as possible. We also want to make sure our money is safe and that it's not going to disappear due to forces beyond our control. We want to have our money follow us through to the end because with it, we can live out our lives in meaningful ways.

It reminds me of a story that's been circulating the internet. The author is unknown, so I can't give credit to any one person for it, but it hits home with what I've been talking about throughout the book. My precious eighty-five-year-old mom, whom you met in Chapter 1, actually emailed this to me.

Here it is:

A professor stood before his philosophy class and had some items in front of him.

When the class began, wordlessly, he picked up a very large and empty mayonnaise jar and filled it with golf balls.

He then asked the students if the jar was full. They agreed that it was.

The professor then picked up a box of pebbles and poured it into the jar. He shook the jar lightly. The pebbles rolled into the open areas between the golf balls.

He then asked the students again if the jar was full. They agreed it was.

The professor next picked up a box of sand and poured it into the jar. Of course, the sand filled up everything else.

> *He asked once more if the jar was full. The students responded with a unanimous "YES." The professor then produced two cups of coffee from under the table and poured the entire contents into the jar, effectively filling the empty space between the sand. The students laughed.*
>
> *"Now," said the professor, as the laughter subsided, "I want you to recognize that this jar represents your life. The golf balls are the important things—faith, family, children, health, friends, and favorite passions. Things that if everything else was lost and only they remained, your life would still be full. The pebbles are the things that matter, like your job, house, and car. The sand is everything else—the small stuff," he said.*
>
> *"If you put the sand into the jar first," he continued, "There is no room for the pebbles or the golf balls. The same goes for life. If you spend all your time and energy on the small stuff, you will never have room for the things that are important to you, he told them.*
>
> *"So pay attention to the things that are critical to your happiness. Worship with your family. Play with your children. Take your partner out to dinner. Spend time with good friends. There will always be time to clean the house and fix the dripping tap. Take care of the golf balls first— the things that really matter. Set your priorities. The rest is just sand."*
>
> *One of the students raised her hand and inquired what the coffee represented.*
>
> *The professor smiled and said, "I'm glad you asked. It just goes to show you that no matter how full your life may seem, there's always room for a couple of cups of coffee with a friend.*

Your money is like the sand. If you concentrate only on it, it can fill your life and leave no room for anything else.

Those things that matter—your health, your relationships, the health of your caretaker, your family, your friends—that's the stuff that needs nurturing. The money is simply there to support the important stuff.

So remember to kiss those you love and tell them how much they mean to you. Do it often. Mend old wounds, give and receive forgiveness. It's worth the effort. Then, when it's your turn to need care, you know you will have the means to do it with grace and dignity. Just as important, the person who chooses to take care of you will do it willingly and ably because you took the time years earlier—even decades to make sure that when the time comes, you can laugh together, tell stories of your younger years, and enjoy those cups of coffee together without worrying about how you're going to pay for it all.

Acknowledgements

THIS BOOK IS THE CULMINATION OF THE LAST FIFTEEN years of my life and work on this topic. Great things are always accomplished through relationships. I don't believe that any of them are by accident. Here are the people that God used to help me write this book and that I want to thank:

Tyrone Clark for having the same vision and commitment to take this message to the world. Your partnership, forty-plus years of experience, off-the-charts creative thinking, and the faith we share in Jesus means the world to me. I look forward to taking this journey together.

Dr. Patricia Ross, for being the amazing editor and publisher you are while living this subject daily with your mom. I knew we were meant to work on this book together. As I saw it unfold, it turned out to be a true labor of love for both of us.

Ronda Taylor, the designer who had to go back to the drawing-board on more than one occasion to get all the pieces to fit together. You made the book look good.

Jim Bowers, my colleague who gave up his time and attention to proofread the galley. His attention to detail is noteworthy.

WHEN RETIREMENT GOES BAD—LIFE SUCKS

Jill, Tyler, Katelyn, and Kian, my precious family, for being patient when Daddy had the door locked and couldn't answer it. (Sorry for hollering from my desk, "I'm working," more than once.) You are more important to me than an ocean full of books or any work.

Kelly Martin and Austin Morris for helping me continue to take great care of our current clients while this project was getting birthed. Your self-motivated work ethic, skilled attention to detail, and consistent encouragement continue to mean so much to me and our success.

Timothy L. Takacs, for your mentoring, friendship, and teaching me "The Rule" and "The Four Lines."

The hundreds of families that entrusted me to help them navigate elder care planning for their loved ones and all of the Care Providers that sent them to come to see me. Without those experiences, I would not have known to look beyond the money to understand the real cost families pay when the money is running out.

About the Author

KERRY MORRIS IS THE FOUNDER of HonorShield, LLC., a firm he launched to challenge the current thinking and behavior of consumers and financial advisors around preparing for the potential high cost of aging.

He has spent several of his twenty-five-year career advising hundreds of families experiencing the nightmare of paying for care. The question, always, was "how to make the money last"? The answer would lead him to discover a whole new way to approach and solve this problem: the LCAP—the Longevity Care Allocation Plan.

Morris learned the value of hard work watching his dad, a truck driver, and his mom, a secretary, provide a solid middle-class childhood for him and his sister in and around Nashville TN in the late 60's and 70's. He got his first job when he was fourteen, making $2.75 an hour taking care of baseball fields, and he's never looked back. As he worked his way through high school and university, playing multiple sports, and then spending almost ten years in the TN National Guard and Army Reserve, he developed a respect for the hard work it took any family to build and maintain a nest egg for their future. He honors those efforts with every plan he builds for his clients.

As a CERTIFIED FINANCIAL PLANNER™ professional, he has watched too many families, too many men and women not be fully prepared for retirement. There had to be a better way, a win-win solution that more American's could feel good about embracing. But there was another problem: he witnessed time and again how the financial industry had this issue on total "ignore" mode, often shoving it onto a small-but valiant band of traditional "insurance specialists" around the country. Less than 10% of Americans have ever embraced this model. That is a problem for American families and our country.

Every person, every family deserves to know how an LCAP works. Kerry Morris has made it his life's goal to ensure that those he helps can hold their head high and know that no matter what curve balls retirement throws at them, they will be prepared.

Contact HonorShield

Find out how you can secure your LCAP.

www.HonorShield.com

www.ingramcontent.com/pod-product-compliance
Lightning Source LLC
Chambersburg PA
CBHW022115090426
42743CB00008B/866